O9-BHJ-142

OUR BEST FRIENDS

The Shih Tzu

OUR BEST FRIENDS

WITHDRAWN
Baldwinsville Public Library
33 East Genesee Street
Baldwinsville, NY 13027-2575

OUR BEST FRIENDS

The Shih Tzu

Karen Schweitzer

ELDORADO INK

Produced by OTTN Publishing, Stockton, New Jersey

Eldorado Ink
PO Box 100097
Pittsburgh, PA 15233
www.eldoradoink.com

Copyright © 2008 by Eldorado Ink. All rights reserved.
Printed and bound in Malaysia.

First printing

1 3 5 7 9 8 6 4 2

Library of Congress Cataloging-in-Publication Data

Schweitzer, Karen.
   The Shih tzu / Karen Schweitzer.
      p. cm. — (Our best friends)
   Includes bibliographical references and index.
   ISBN-13: 978-1-932904-25-3 (hc)
   ISBN-10: 1-932904-25-5 (hc)
   1. Shih tzu. I. Title.
   SF429.S64S39 2008
   636.76—dc22
                                        2007044879
   JUN 0 6 2011

Photo credits: © American Animal Hospital Association, 43; © iStockphoto.com/Jeff
Dalton: 67; © iStockphoto.com/Sojna Foos: 71; © iStockphoto.com/Shannon Long: 49,
60; © iStockphoto.com/Mike McCune: 22; © iStockphoto.com/Denise McQuillen: 102;
© iStockphoto.com/James Pauls: 82; © iStockphoto.com/Purdue9394: 108;
© iStockphoto.com/Ludovic Rhodes: 85, 87; © 2008 Jupiterimages Corporation, 27, 98;
courtesy National Association of Professional Pet Sitters, www.petsitters.org: 89; used
under license from Shutterstock, Inc.: 3, 8, 10, 15, 16, 19, 21, 23, 25, 28, 30, 32, 33, 36,
38, 39, 40, 41, 45, 47, 52, 55, 59, 62, 64, 65, 72, 74, 76, 80, 90; 93; 95; 103; 106, front
cover (all), back cover.

TABLE OF CONTENTS

Introduction

GARY KORSGAARD, DVM

The mutually beneficial relationship between humans and animals began long before the dawn of recorded history. Archaeologists believe that humans began to capture and tame wild goats, sheep, and pigs more than 9,000 years ago. These animals were then bred for specific purposes, such as providing humans with a reliable source of food or providing furs and hides that could be used for clothing or the construction of dwellings.

Other animals had been sought for companionship and assistance even earlier. The dog, believed to be the first animal domesticated, began living and working with Stone Age humans in Europe more than 14,000 years ago. Some archaeologists believe that wild dogs and humans were drawn together because both hunted the same prey. By taming and training dogs, humans became more effective hunters. Dogs, meanwhile, enjoyed the social contact with humans and benefited from greater access to food and warm shelter. Dogs soon became beloved pets as well as trusted workers. This can be seen from the many artifacts depicting dogs that have been found at ancient sites in Asia, Europe, North America, and the Middle East.

The earliest domestic cats appeared in the Middle East about 5,000 years ago. Small wild cats were probably first attracted to human settlements because plenty of rodents could be found wherever harvested grain was stored. Cats played a useful role in hunting and killing these pests, and it is likely that grateful humans rewarded them for this assistance. Over time, these small cats gave up some of their aggressive wild behaviors and began living among humans. Cats eventually became so popular in ancient Egypt that they were believed to possess magical powers. Cat statues were placed outside homes to ward off evil spirits, and mummified cats were included in royal tombs to accompany their owners into the afterlife.

Today, few people believe that cats have supernatural powers, but most pet owners feel a magical bond with their pets, whether they are dogs, cats, hamsters, rabbits, horses, or parrots. The lives of pets and their people become inextricably intertwined, providing strong emotional and physical rewards for both humans and animals. People of all ages can benefit from the loving companionship of a pet. Not surprisingly, then, pet ownership is widespread. Recent statistics indicate that about 60 percent of all households in the United States and Canada have at least one pet, while the figure is close to 50 percent of households in the United Kingdom. For millions of people, therefore, pets truly have become their "best friends."

Finding the best animal friend can be a challenge, however. Not only are there many types of domesticated pets, but each has specific needs, characteristics, and personality traits. Even within a category of pets, such as dogs, different breeds will flourish in different surroundings and with different treatment. For example, a German Shepherd may not be the right pet for a person living in a cramped urban apartment; that person might be better off caring for a smaller dog like a Toy Poodle or Shih Tzu, or perhaps a cat. On the other hand, an active person who loves the outdoors may prefer the companionship of a Labrador Retriever to that of a small dog or a passive indoor pet like a goldfish or hamster.

The joys of pet ownership come with certain responsibilities. Bringing a pet into your home and your neighborhood obligates you to care for and train the pet properly. For example, a dog must be housebroken, taught to obey your commands, and trained to behave appropriately when he encounters other people or animals. Owners must also be mindful of their pet's particular nutritional and medical needs.

The purpose of the OUR BEST FRIENDS series is to provide a helpful and comprehensive introduction to pet ownership. Each book contains the basic information a prospective pet owner needs in order to choose the right pet for his or her situation and to care for that pet throughout the pet's lifetime. Training, socialization, proper nutrition, potential medical issues, and the legal responsibilities of pet ownership are thoroughly explained and discussed, and an abundance of expert tips and suggestions are offered. Whether it is a hamster, corn snake, guinea pig, or Labrador Retriever, the books in the OUR BEST FRIENDS series provide everything the reader needs to know about how to have a happy, well-adjusted, and well-behaved pet.

CHAPTER ONE

Is a Shih Tzu Right for You?

Are you dazzled by the Shih Tzu's expressive eyes and glorious coat? You're not alone. According to the number of new registrations received by the American Kennel Club (AKC) on an annual basis, the Shih Tzu is among the most popular breeds.

These dogs are appealing for a number of reasons. The Shih Tzu is relatively small in stature, but is very strong and sturdy and has few health problems. Dogs of this breed are also considered to be extremely intelligent, and will use their ingenuity to find ways to entertain themselves, and you. Shih Tzus are active, friendly, and independent. Typically, they are not aggressive and usually get along well with children and other animals. To say that the Shih Tzu is a "people dog" is in no way an exaggeration. Members of this breed love spending time with their owners and can be very affectionate.

But as lovable as the Shih Tzu is, this breed may not be right for everyone. It takes a lot of work—in most cases, daily grooming—to keep the Shih Tzu's long coat beautiful and tangle free. If the hair gets matted, it's very difficult to untangle. Coat care for the Shih Tzu requires such dedication that it must be carefully considered by anyone who may be interested in this breed.

This dog should also be avoided if you're looking for a guard dog.

Although the average Shih Tzu is very alert, dogs of this breed are not "yappy," and are much more likely to show an intruder around the house than to scare him away.

PHYSICAL CHARACTERISTICS

Physically, the Shih Tzu is a beauty. The breed is small in size, ideally weighing between 9 and 16 pounds (4–7 kg). Like most toy breeds, the Shih Tzu is long-backed with an arrogant stance. There are, however, two striking features that set this breed apart. The first is the delightful expression created by the Shih Tzu's chrysanthemum-like face, and the second is the glorious double coat.

The double coat is usually kept long, so that it almost brushes the ground as the Shih Tzu walks. While most dogs have fur, the Shih Tzu actually has hair similar to a human's. A Shih Tzu, therefore, does not shed seasonally like other dogs, but rather loses hair gradually, as humans do.

Shih Tzus come in many different colors, and have many different markings on their coat. No one color or marking pattern is thought to be better than another, and all are permissible in AKC purebred shows. Some of the most common colors that can be found in a Shih Tzu's coat include white and red,

Purebred Shih Tzus come in a variety of colors.

white and gold, white and black, white and silver, and brindle (a mix of gold or silver and black).

A SHIH TZU'S ROLE IN YOUR LIFE

A Shih Tzu can play many roles in a dog owner's life, but this dog's favorite role, and the one he was bred for, is that of companion. A Shih Tzu loves to be close to his owner, and takes more pleasure in that than anything else.

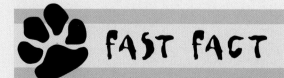

FAST FACT

It's very rare to see a Shih Tzu with an all-white coat. Most have colored markings somewhere.

But there are many other parts the Shih Tzu can play in your life. Many dedicated owners enjoy training and showing their Shih Tzus. This does, however, take a fair amount of determination; Shih Tzus can be stubborn, which means obedience training can quickly turn into a battle of wills.

There is also the option of breeding a Shih Tzu. This too takes a great amount of determination, as well as a love of the breed itself. Experienced breeders sometimes take years developing bloodlines and finding the perfect dogs to breed.

THE BEST ENVIRONMENT FOR YOUR SHIH TZU

Although the Shih Tzu is considered to be a hardy dog, and is very good with children, this breed is small in size. For this reason alone, a Shih Tzu may not make a good pet for young children who have not yet learned the proper way to handle a dog. Shih Tzu puppies are very deli-

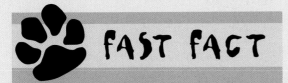

FAST FACT

Before acquiring a Shih Tzu, you must be prepared to make a long-term commitment. The typical Shih Tzu has a life expectancy of 14 to 16 years.

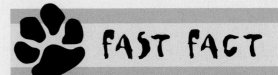

FAST FACT

In recent years, the Shih Tzu has become such a popular breed that it consistently ranks among the top 10 breeds in the United States and currently stands at number 12 in the United Kingdom.

cate. They need to be treated with compassion and gentleness so that they are not frightened or injured.

The best environment for a Shih Tzu is one with a kind companion or a family in which he would receive regular attention. Of course, this does not mean that Shih Tzus need to be supervised 24 hours a day. Left to their own devices, most will sleep or find a way to amuse themselves. However, if left alone for too long, dogs of this breed will pine for their owners.

Luckily, the Shih Tzu travels well, and most owners find that they can take their pet with them almost everywhere. If you do need to leave home for a substantial period, and can't take your Shih Tzu with you, boarding is always an option, as is leaving your dog with a relative or asking someone to watch your dog in familiar surroundings.

It should also be noted that the Shih Tzu adapts well to change, and

FAST FACT

The American Kennel Club designates groups that include a number of breeds with similar characteristics. According to AKC registrations, the Shih Tzu is the most popular member of the "toy group," which also includes other smaller dogs like the Chihuahua and the Yorkshire Terrier.

can be happy almost anywhere. Because of its small size, this dog is a wonderful option for people who live in apartments or tight quarters. A Shih Tzu is also good for owners who don't have time to take long daily walks. Although Shih Tzus enjoy exercise and aren't opposed to romps in the park, this breed doesn't need the vigorous activity that some dogs require. A Shih Tzu can get all the exercise he needs by playing with toys, following his owner, or taking short jaunts around the block.

BASIC COSTS ASSOCIATED WITH SHIH TZU OWNERSHIP

Owning any type of dog comes with great responsibility, some of which is financial. When it comes to owning a Shih Tzu, there is the purchase price to consider, as well as the other costs associated with pet ownership. In the first year alone,

you may spend anywhere from $300 to $2,500, so it's important to be prepared ahead of time.

The total amount you pay out-of-pocket will depend on several things, including how healthy your dog is and how much you like to spoil your pooch. That said, there are basic costs for which every Shih Tzu owner is responsible. Knowing what these costs are beforehand and analyzing whether or not you can afford them could save you a great deal of heartache later on.

ROUTINE VETERINARY CARE: After bringing your new Shih Tzu home, you'll need to have the dog examined by a qualified veterinarian. The cost for this varies, depending on the vet and the thoroughness of the examination. In most cases, you can expect to pay between $15 and $200. After the initial examination,

FAST FACT

While it is a good idea to budget for routine vet bills, you may also want to have an emergency fund on hand in case your Shih Tzu has an accident or an unexpected illness. Some vets will not allow you to charge visits on a credit card, but instead require cash.

you'll need to return at least once each year for a wellness exam.

IMMUNIZATIONS: Shih Tzu puppies require a series of vaccinations for distemper, hepatitis, leptospirosis, parainfluenza, and parvovirus (DHLPP). By six months old, puppies need a rabies shot. At 16 months old, the dog will need another DHLPP shot, and another rabies shot. Every year after that, your Shih Tzu will need a DHLPP booster shot; he'll also need regular rabies boosters. There are also vaccinations for Lyme disease, kennel cough, and other illnesses. Your vet will be able to recommend which shots your Shih Tzu needs, and will also be able to set up a schedule for the vaccinations. The cost of immunization depends on the vet, but generally falls between $15 and $150 annually.

PARASITE TESTS AND PREVENTION: Internal parasites, like tapeworms, roundworms, hookworms, and heartworms, can make your Shih Tzu very ill. Your vet will need to test your dog for parasites every year and if necessary provide medication that can kill or prevent worms. The cost of the annual tests and medication vary, but will most likely run at least $25 per year.

FLEA AND TICK PREVENTION: Fleas and ticks are a dog's worst enemy. Fleas can damage your Shih Tzu's

BUYING A SHIH TZU TO BREED

Many people consider breeding a pet Shih Tzu to make back the money they spent purchasing the dog. However, this is generally not a good idea. Breeding is a huge responsibility, and can prove to be an expensive venture. A Shih Tzu needs to be checked for diseases and infections—both inherited and otherwise—before being bred. There is also the expense of caring for puppies after they are born.

It's not unusual for a conscientious Shih Tzu breeder to spend more money on breeding, whelping, and raising a litter of puppies than can be recouped from the sale of those puppies. In other words, it can be very difficult to break even, let alone make a decent return on the time and money you have invested in the project. If you're thinking about breeding Shih Tzus, you should do so for the love of the breed, rather than for profit.

skin and coat, and may cause ane-mia, hair loss, or allergic reactions. Ticks are equally irksome, albeit more dangerous, as they can carry Lyme disease. Preventing fleas and ticks can be expensive, but treating them is even more costly. Fortunately, there are many good prevention products on the market that your vet can recommend. The annual cost for these products varies, depending on the area in which you live and the product you use, but the average annual cost should be some-where around $50 to $100.

SPAYING OR NEUTERING: Unless you plan on breeding your Shih Tzu, it's a good idea to spay or neuter your dog around the age of six months. This will prevent unwanted pregnancies, undesirable behavior, and life-threatening health issues like mammary cancer and pyometra (an infected uterus). The one-time cost of spaying or neutering averages $50 to $250.

GROOMING SUPPLIES: You'll need a whole collection of grooming sup-plies to care for your Shih Tzu's coat. Required supplies include a pin brush, a steel comb, and a dematting tool. If you plan to bathe and trim

FAST FACT

If you love your Shih Tzu, but don't have time to groom him daily, you can keep your Shih Tzu's coat trimmed short. This hairstyle, known as a pet trim or a puppy cut, is much easier to maintain.

your pet at home, you'll need addi-tional equipment. Again, the exact cost will vary depending on what you buy and where you shop.

TOYS: Toys are an absolute must for Shih Tzus of all ages. If you don't give your pet something to play with, your personal possessions will turn into his source of amusement. There is no limit to the amount you can spend on toys, but you should plan on buying at least $20 worth of qual-ity toys every year.

FOOD AND MISCELLANEOUS SUPPLIES: There are a number of other supplies you'll need to care for your Shih Tzu. These include, but are not limited to, a crate, bedding, a collar, a leash, dog bowls, and treats. Plan to spend upwards from $200 to $2,000 on these items.

CHAPTER TWO

Shih Tzu History and Breed Standard

Although many people associate the Shih Tzu with China, Tibet is considered to be the ancestral home of this little dog. Shih Tzus are descended from the Tibetan Lhasa Apso, a dog held in very high esteem among Tibetan nobles. The Lhasa Apso is one of several breeds collectively known as Tibetan Lion Dogs. These dogs were frequently presented as gifts in exchange for safe passage from Tibet to other countries.

The Shih Tzu is believed to be descended from Lhasa Apso dogs (pictured above), originally found in Tibet.

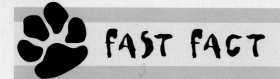

FAST FACT

Loosely translated, Shih Tzu (pronounced SHEED-Zoo) means "lion" in Chinese.

THE SHIH TZU IN CHINA

The exact origin of the Shih Tzu is obscure, and there are various theories as to when the dog's ancestors arrived in China. The most common theory has ancestors of the Shih Tzu coming to China in 1650 during the Qing dynasty. Little dogs were very popular in China at this time, and were accorded honored places in the Chinese court.

Of course, there is also the story of the Dowager Empress Tsu Hsi. In 1908, the dowager empress received several small dogs as a gift from the Dalai Lama. She fondly referred to them as her "Shih Tzu Kou," or "lion dogs." In an effort to maintain the special breed characteristics of her beloved Shih Tzu Kou, the dowager empress kept the dogs separate from the more than 100 Pekinese she owned. Whether or not this plan worked is unknown. The empress died not long after receiving the treasured gifts from the Dalai Lama, and the responsibility of breeding and keeping the Shih Tzu Kou was left to the palace eunuchs.

THE SHIH TZU IN BRITAIN

The Shih Tzu arrived in Britain from China in 1930. Several notable British breeders took an interest in the majestic little dog, and in 1933 the Shih Tzu made its debut at the West of England Kennel Club Show. (At the time, the breed went by the name Apso rather than Shih Tzu.)

It was at this show that the judge, famed Apsos importer Colonel

The Chinese nicknamed Shih Tzus "lion dogs" because of their mane-like facial hair.

FAST FACT

There are many old Chinese paintings and other objects d'art featuring dogs that look extraordinarily like the Shih Tzu. These pieces date back as far as A.D. 624.

Frederick M. Bailey, expressed his belief that there were notable differences between the "lion dogs" being exhibited. This sparked a great debate that was eventually resolved when the decision was made to separate the dogs from China (Shih Tzu) and the dogs from Tibet (Lhasa Apso).

THE SHIH TZU IN THE UNITED STATES

In the mid-1930s, the first Shih Tzus were imported from England to the United States. Once again, members of the breed were mistakenly identified as Lhasa Apsos at first. The American Kennel Club did not correct this error until 1950, by which time a great deal of crossbreeding between Lhasa Apsos and Shih Tzus had occurred. This breeding, along with the crossing of Scandinavian and English imports, led to the American Shih Tzu we know and love today.

Although the Shih Tzu's rise to popularity was perhaps delayed by the initial confusion over the name, the dog quickly garnered nationwide interest. The breed was admitted to the American Kennel Club's Miscellaneous Class in 1955.

In 1963, the American Shih Tzu Club was formed. This club maintained a stud book and did a great deal to promote the breed in the United States. Six years later, the Shih Tzu was admitted to registration in the American Kennel Club Stud Book. Today, the Shih Tzu is one of America's best-loved breeds.

THE SHIH TZU IN OTHER COUNTRIES

Shih Tzus were imported to many other countries at the same time that the breed came to the United States. In 1935, the first Shih Tzus were registered in Canada and—you guessed it—were originally mistaken for another breed: the Lhasa Terrier. This error was eventually corrected, and today there is virtually no difference between breed standards established by the American Kennel Club

FAST FACT

Alternate names for the Shih Tzu are Chinese Lion Dog, Tibetan Lion Dog, Shock Dog, and Chrysanthemum Dog.

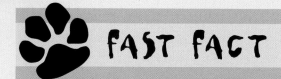

FAST FACT

The American Kennel Club did not recognize the Shih Tzu as a separate breed until the 1950s. Prior to that, Shih Tzus were shown as Lhasa Apsos.

and those established by the Canadian Kennel Club.

The Shih Tzu came to Norway in 1932, to Sweden and France in 1950, to Finland in 1955, and to Germany in 1960. There are many enthusiastic clubs and organizations in these countries dedicated to the Shih Tzu. Other countries where the breed is popular include Japan, Mexico, Australia, Thailand, and Czechoslovakia.

HOW YESTERDAY'S LION DOGS INFLUENCED TODAY'S SHIH TZU

Unlike some dogs, Shih Tzus were not necessarily bred for sporting or guarding purposes. This ornamental breed was meant to be a status symbol and a prized companion with no real utilitarian purpose. As palace pets, Shih Tzus lived a life of luxury. They drank antelope milk, dined on delicacies like shark fin and rhinoceros horn, and even received massages.

The original purpose of the Shih Tzu had a clear impact on the breed's temperament and behavior. Today, Shih Tzus have a distinctly arrogant carriage and typically thrive in the role of companion. Most Shih Tzus love to be pampered, and would follow their owners anywhere simply for the company.

BREED STANDARDS AND CONFORMATION

The American Kennel Club, which sets the official breed standard for dogs in the United States, describes the Shih Tzu as a "sturdy, lively, alert toy dog with a long flowing double coat." AKC also notes that while there is "considerable size variation" among dogs of this breed, Shih Tzus must be "compact, solid, carrying good weight and substance."

Shih Tzus that don't meet AKC standards can make wonderful pets and companions, but it should be noted that dogs that don't conform are not eligible to participate in any AKC-sanctioned Conformation shows. In addition, for obvious reasons, they are not good dogs to use for breeding prospective champions. Some of the standards established by AKC are as follows:

SIZE: The weight of a mature Shih Tzu should fall somewhere between 9 and 16 pounds (four and seven kg). The ideal height of a fully grown

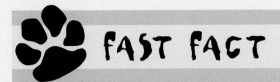

FAST FACT

When purchasing a Shih Tzu, don't be confused by terms like imperial or teacup. These are not different Shih Tzu breeds, but descriptions used for under-sized dogs that don't conform to the official breed standard.

Shih Tzu at the withers (shoulders) is 9 to 10.5 inches (23 to 26.5 cm). In any case, the height should be less than 11 inches (28 cm), but more than 8 inches (20 cm).

STRUCTURE: Proportions are also very important. Shih Tzus should be longer than they are tall, which means dogs should never be so tall that they appear "leggy" or so short and squat that they appear "dumpy." The shoulders should fit smoothly into the body, and hindquarters and forequarters should always be in balance. No one feature of the neck, topline, or body should be exaggerated.

MUZZLE: Shih Tzus should have a short, square muzzle approximately one inch (2.5 cm) in length from the stop to the tip of the nose. Muzzles with down-turns, wrinkles, receding chins, pro-truding chins, and lack of cushion-ing are considered undesirable. Undershot and level bites are acceptable.

NOSE: Liver-pigmented Shih Tzus have dark-liver noses, blue-pigmented

When choosing a Shih Tzu puppy, keep the breed standard in mind if you plan to show your dog.

Shih Tzus have blue noses, and all other Shih Tzus have black noses. Unbroken pigmentation is best. In any case, the nose should be level with the lower eye rims or tilted upward slightly.

EYES: The eyes of a Shih Tzu should be large and round, but not necessarily prominent. Liver-pigmented and blue-pigmented dogs tend to have lighter eyes; extraordinarily dark eyes are the standard for all other Shih Tzus.

EARS: Shih Tzus should have large, heavy-coated ears that are set just below the crown of the skull. Ears should not be prominent, but rather blend in with the hair on the neck.

TAIL: The tail should be set high and curve well into the back. A heavily plumed tail is the standard; any deviation is undesirable.

COAT: Although a very slight wave is permissible, curly hair is not. The Shih Tzu's well-groomed coat should be long and flowing. A double coat is the standard, as is tying the hair on the top of the head into a topknot.

COLOR: Shih Tzus come in many colors; all are permissible, and no

COMMON FAULTS

In the show ring, deviation from the standards established by the American Kennel Club can result in penalties, the extent of which depends heavily on the judge as well as the severity of the deviation. Shih Tzus with too many of these faults may not even be eligible to compete in some AKC events and competitions. According to AKC breed standards for Shih Tzu, common faults include:

- Too scrawny
- Too heavy
- Too leggy
- Squatness
- Narrow head
- Close-set eyes
- Pink coloring on eye rims, nose, or lips
- Down-pointed nose
- Pinched nostrils
- Overshot bite
- Insufficient neck
- Curly coat
- Low-set tail

color is considered superior to others. This is true of markings as well.

MALE VERSUS FEMALE: There are slight distinctions between male and female Shih Tzus, which appear mainly in the head. Shih Tzu bitches have smaller heads than their male counterparts, and tend to exhibit what is known among judges as a "more feminine" expression.

ADDITIONAL NOTES ON THE BREED STANDARD

In most cases, there is very little difference between the standards set by various kennel clubs. It's not unusual for the same Shih Tzu to win both American and Canadian titles. That said, breed standards can vary from country to country. Different judges will also view the same dog a little differently. The Shih Tzu that one judge considers a champion may be bypassed without comment by another judge.

For this reason, Shih Tzu owners who are interested in showing their dogs should do their best to learn as much as possible about the finer points of the breed. Good places to start are established breed clubs. Organizations like the American Shih Tzu Club often have seminars and shows that allow owners, breeders, and exhibitors to get together and learn from one another.

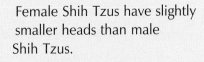

Female Shih Tzus have slightly smaller heads than male Shih Tzus.

CHAPTER THREE

Responsible Shih Tzu Ownership

Owning a Shih Tzu comes with a great deal of responsibility. But there are other basic responsibilities associated with dog ownership that you need to think about as well. For example, it's up to you to make sure your dog doesn't become a nuisance to others. Your neighbors will become very angry and may even call the police if you allow your Shih

Owning a Shih Tzu is much like having a child. His or her well-being is your responsibility. You will be held accountable for any damage or trouble your dog may cause.

Tzu to bark constantly, eliminate on other people's yards, or growl at neighborhood children.

When this happens, you can't blame it on the dog. If your Shih Tzu gets loose and causes a car accident, it's your fault. If your Shih Tzu impregnates a neighbor's dog or bites a child, it's your fault. You're responsible for everything your Shih Tzu does.

IDENTIFICATION

Thousands of pets go missing each year and are not returned, merely because they have no form of identification. It's imperative for you to make it simple for someone who finds your lost Shih Tzu to identify you as the owner. This can be done easily by making your dog wear a collar and/or a pet tag that includes your name and telephone number.

In some areas, dogs in a public place are required to wear a collar or tag that also includes the address and ZIP code of the owner. If the place where you live does not require this, you don't necessarily need to include your name. To discourage someone from stealing your dog, or to encourage prompt return of a lost pet, you may want to add something like "requires medication."

Other identification options include more permanent techniques like tattooing and microchip implantation. Both procedures can be performed at your local veterinary clinic, and neither is particularly painful for your Shih Tzu.

Tattooing is the older of the two techniques. If you choose this method of permanent identification, your dog will have a series of numbers tattooed on his body. The inside of the thigh is the most common spot, but other areas—from the belly to the ears—can be marked as well. The tattoo can contain your telephone number or your dog's AKC registration number.

Although owners have been tattooing their dogs for years, there are problems with this identification technique. The tattoo may fade or become unreadable over time, which

It's a good idea to get a collar with sturdy fasteners to ensure that it doesn't fall off your dog.

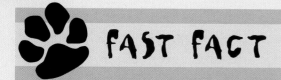

FAST FACT

Tattooing your Shih Tzu can deter professional thieves. Most dog brokers and laboratories will not buy tattooed animals.

means it may have to be redone. Another drawback is that there are several different dog registries. You'll need to register your dog and his contact information with each one as soon as the tattoo is finished.

Microchip implantation is a more modern permanent identification technique. The microchip is actually a computer chip, about the size of a grain of rice, that is implanted in your dog painlessly via an injection. Each chip includes a unique number. If your Shih Tzu does get lost or stolen, and is brought to a veterinary clinic or shelter anywhere in North America, the staff should be able to scan the dog's back with a special microchip reader. Your contact information will come up and you'll be contacted and reunited with your pet.

The major drawback to microchip implantation is that there are several chips and scanners on the market, and not all of them are compatible. There have also been reports of some chips moving around in the

body, as opposed to staying in the spot where they were first implanted. If that happens, a microchip scanner may not be able to read the chip properly.

The best method is to use two forms of identification for your pet. If your Shih Tzu has a tag and a tattoo, a tattoo and a microchip, or a microchip and a tag, the chances of being reunited with your missing pet are much greater.

LICENSING REQUIREMENTS

Every municipality in the United States requires pet owners to register their dogs. In most cases, an annual license must be purchased. You can usually get a license from your local courthouse. In some states, you may be able to purchase a license directly from your veterinarian.

The fee for licensing your Shih Tzu will vary depending on where you live, as well as other factors. Some cities offer you a discount if you have spayed or neutered your pet, or if your dog has permanent identification, like a tattoo or a microchip.

If you fail to get a license for your Shih Tzu, you'll probably be subject to a stiff fine. In some areas, not licensing your dog is considered a misdemeanor offense. To save yourself any trouble, you should abide by the law and purchase a new license for your dog each year.

SPAYING OR NEUTERING YOUR SHIH TZU

Unless you plan to show or breed your Shih Tzu, spaying or neutering your pet is the responsible thing to do. Spaying (females) or neutering (males) helps your pet to live a longer and healthier life. Females that have been spayed are less likely to develop uterine, ovarian, and breast cancer. Males that have been neutered are less likely to develop testicular cancer or suffer from prostate disease.

The other, more obvious benefit of spaying or neutering your pet is the prevention of unwanted puppies.

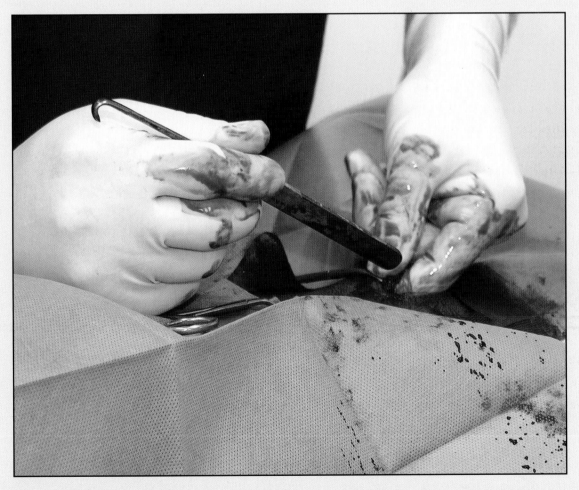

For most Shih Tzu owners, spaying or neutering is a wise decision. These procedures not only eliminate the possibility of unwanted puppies, they also provide health benefits for your dog.

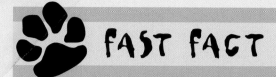

FAST FACT

Your Shih Tzu may have to stay one or two nights at the vet's office after being spayed or neutered. The length of the stay is usually determined by your pet's age, size, and health, as well as the vet's standard policy.

Every year, thousands of dogs are abandoned at shelters and pounds. Many of these dogs are never adopted, and are eventually put to death. Make sure you don't add to these already horrendous statistics by spaying or neutering your pet as soon as possible.

Shih Tzus can be spayed or neutered at six months of age. Most vets suggest spaying a female before her first heat cycle. Both surgeries are relatively inexpensive. If properly medicated, your Shih Tzu will experience minimal pain.

Don't worry that spaying or neutering your pet will change your pet for the worse. It's a myth that sterilizing a dog changes his temperament or personality. Instead, spaying or neutering your Shih Tzu will make your dog a better, more affectionate pet, and will almost always eliminate unwanted behaviors, like mounting and roaming.

PET INSURANCE

People insure their cars, their homes, and, sometimes, even their pets. Pet insurance has been available for 20 years, and is becoming more popular as more pet owners recognize the importance of good veterinary care.

Policies can be purchased almost anywhere. An online search will yield dozens and dozens of companies that offer health and life insurance plans for pets. You can also get recommendations from your veterinarian. However, every pet insurance plan is different, so it's a good idea to research and compare several plans before making any final decisions. Specific things to compare include the level of coverage being offered, monthly or annual rates, copays, and deductibles.

Most plans cover accidents, illnesses, and serious medical

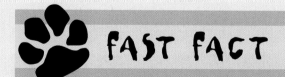

FAST FACT

Some pet insurance plans don't cover congenital and hereditary conditions associated with the Shih Tzu breed. Ask your pet insurance carrier for a list of exclusions before you purchase a policy.

Not all pet insurance policies cover the same things. Before you sign on the dotted line, do research and make an informed decision.

problems. There are an increasing number of carriers that also provide coverage for preventative care, such as annual checkups, teeth cleaning, heartworm and flea control, spaying or neutering, and some health screenings, such as testing for parasites. The policies that include preventative care coverage tend to cost a little more, so do the math and make sure the insurance plan makes financial sense for you.

You should also find out about procedures and conditions that are not covered. Every policy has exclusions. For example, many will not pay for preexisting conditions, or for elective procedures like teeth cleaning.

A final factor worth considering is the way various insurance carriers pay out a claim. Some will pay your veterinarian directly, while others require you to pay upfront, fill out a claim form, and get reimbursed at a later date.

COMMON LEGAL ISSUES

Your Shih Tzu can easily get you into trouble with the law if you're not careful. Most towns and cities have local noise ordinances that may be violated by your barking pet. The punishment often depends on where you live, but you can usually expect a citation and a fine.

Not picking up after your Shih Tzu can also get you into hot water. If you're walking your dog, be sure

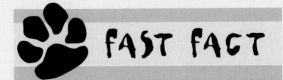

FAST FACT

Be responsible when walking your Shih Tzu. Keep him on a leash at all times, and clean up after him immediately if he makes a mess.

Be respectful of your neighbors. Picking up after your Shih Tzu when he "does his business" in public areas and keeping him from barking excessively is not only considerate, it is required by law in many communities.

to clean up any messes he might leave behind. The fines for not doing so can be considerable.

WHEN YOUR PET BITES

According to the Centers for Disease Control and Prevention, dogs bite more than 4.7 million people in the United States each year. Medical treatment is required in more than 800,000 cases. Half of the people treated are children.

If your Shih Tzu is aggressive, you must take precautions to make sure that nobody gets bitten. Keep your dog away from children, post signs on your property, and warn visitors about the potential danger the moment they enter your house or yard. You may also want to seek out a trainer or

LIABILITY INSURANCE

The cost of the average dog bite claim exceeds $20,000. This is a huge expense for any pet owner. Fortunately, many homeowner's insurance policies, and even some renter's policies, typically cover dog bite liability. If you have a dog, check your policy to make sure you're covered in the event of an accident.

If you're not covered by your current insurance policy, you can purchase umbrella insurance or dog liability insurance from a number of carriers that specialize in liability or pet insurance coverage. As with any insurance, the rates and terms may vary greatly, depending on the provider. Be sure to check around to get the best coverage and the best price. You can usually get free quotes online or by making a few phone calls to insurance agents in your area.

behavior specialist to find out how you can further control, and hopefully correct, your pet's unacceptable behavior.

It's your responsibility to make sure that your Shih Tzu does not bite a person or another animal. If he does, you'll be held responsible. The legal ramifications can be serious and, depending on the severity of the bite, expensive.

Lawsuits are very common in today's society, but if you're considerate of other people, and take precautions to protect yourself, it should be relatively easy to keep yourself and your Shih Tzu out of trouble.

CHAPTER FOUR

The Best Possible Beginning

If you have seen a Shih Tzu in the show ring, in the home of a friend or family member, or even in pictures, then you already know how easy it is to get drawn in by this adorable little dog. However, it's important to realize that pet ownership is one of the biggest responsibilities you'll ever undertake. This is especially true with Shih Tzu ownership.

When you bring your trusting new friend home, you'll be committing yourself to approximately 15 years of responsibility. It will be your job to care for your dog to the best of your ability—in good times

When choosing a Shih Tzu, consider your family, lifestyle, and the size of your home. Doing research and making an informed choice will be best for everyone.

and bad. Although Shih Tzus live to please their owners, this doesn't mean that they won't get themselves into trouble every now and then.

CHOOSING A DOG

Once you're confident that you're ready for the responsibility of a pet and have decided that a Shih Tzu is the right dog for you and your family, the next step will be choosing a dog. This process will be much easier if you know what role your new Shih Tzu will play in your life. For example, if you're looking for a show dog, your search criteria will be a little different than those of someone seeking a companion animal.

Show dogs must meet the breed standards established by the American Kennel Club if they are going to be shown in the United States, or the breed standards of appropriate clubs if they will be shown in other countries. Companion dogs, on the other hand, only need to live up to your personal standards. This doesn't mean that you shouldn't search for a healthy dog or a dog with a good temperament; it simply means you don't have to worry as much if your new pet's parents have close-set eyes or a long nose.

MALES VERSUS FEMALES

Think Shih Tzu females have a better temperament than males? You're not alone. Breeders report more requests for females than for males. But the truth is that gender isn't as important as bloodlines when it comes to the Shih Tzu breed. Both dogs and bitches are affectionate little creatures, and neither sex is known for being overly aggressive.

Males are sometimes the preferred sex for pet owners who show Shih Tzus, simply because males don't suffer the periodic, hormone-related coat loss that is common among females. However, neither gender is considered superior in the show ring.

SHIH TZU PUPPIES

Deciding between a Shih Tzu puppy and an adult dog can be difficult. There are advantages and disadvantages to each choice. If you buy a puppy, you can raise the pup yourself; this guarantees that your dog will know what is and isn't permitted in a

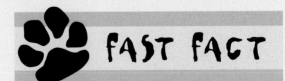

FAST FACT

Shih Tzus come in a variety of colors, but according to the American Shih Tzu Club, breeders say the most highly requested color combination is gold and white.

Shih Tzu puppies are so delicate that extra care must be taken to ensure they aren't injured as they grow.

given situation. You also get the joy of raising your pet from an itty-bitty pup to a full-fledged adult dog, an experience that can be very rewarding.

Then again, puppies aren't for everyone. Shih Tzu puppies are very tiny, weighing only four to six ounces (113 to 170 grams) at birth. Patience and a gentle hand are required in the training process to ensure that the puppy is not frightened or accidentally injured. While most Shih Tzu puppies have a deep desire to please their owners, they'll make mischief frequently during the first year or two.

There is also the issue of housebreaking. If you have a busy or erratic schedule, you may not have the time you need to devote to this crucial task. Puppies that are left cooped up too long will most certainly have accidents, and if you aren't there to take them out frequently or correct their mistakes, this behavior can become very hard to break.

ADULT SHIH TZUS

If your schedule doesn't mesh with the needs of a Shih Tzu puppy, or if you're interested in owning a show dog, a fully mature Shih Tzu is probably the way to go. When you buy an adult dog, what you see is generally what you get. This is especially important if you want to show your Shih Tzu, as you'll easily be able to tell whether or not the dog conforms to the established breed standards.

Of course, looks are just about the only thing you can be sure of when getting an adult dog. Temperament is often very dependent on how the Shih Tzu was socialized as a puppy. You may be able to get an idea of what a dog is like by handling him and asking questions before making the purchase, but that doesn't mean you won't get any surprises later.

Older dogs not used to being around children or other pets may find it stressful to suddenly be thrust into a household with three kids and a cat. If the dog was abused or poorly trained as a puppy, there is also a chance of behavioral

There are plenty of adult Shih Tzus in need of loving homes. You can find great dogs at local shelters or rescue agencies.

issues surfacing once you take your new pet home. Such problems can be trying, but not impossible to work though. Shih Tzus are among the most adaptable dog breeds on the planet. An adult Shih Tzu brought into a loving home will almost certainly thrive, particularly if the humans around him are patient and considerate enough to ease the transition.

FINDING A BREEDER

Once you've decided that you want a Shih Tzu, your first instinct might be to turn to the newspaper or the guy down the street who frequently has a sign out in his yard advertising "puppies for sale." This might not be the best way to go, because backyard

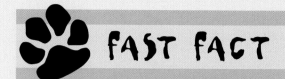

Not sure where to get your puppy? Contact the American, UK, or Canadian kennel clubs. These organizations can refer you to a breeder or national breed club.

breeders are not guaranteed to be reputable.

You'll be better off if you find a breeder through an established source like a breed club or a kennel club. Breeders who are registered with an established club are more likely to be knowledgeable about the breed, and much more likely to be in the business for the love of Shih Tzus as opposed to the love of money. Most important, registered breeders typically choose bloodlines carefully to achieve the desired temperament and maintain the breed standard, which increases your chances of purchasing a happy and healthy pup.

ATTRIBUTES OF A REPUTABLE BREEDER

There are a lot of Shih Tzu breeders out there, but not all of them can be considered reputable. That's why it pays to learn as much about a breeder as possible before purchasing a puppy. Specific attributes to look for include the following:

Buyer Beware: It's not wise to purchase a Shih Tzu from a "puppy mill"—a kennel where large numbers of dogs are bred in unhealthy conditions. Many of the dogs that come from these mills have not been socialized or cared for properly. Before you pick up your puppy, take a good look around the breeder's property. Is it clean? Are the dogs well fed and well cared for? You should be able to answer yes to both of these questions.

EXPERIENCE: An experienced breeder is generally a knowledgeable breeder. If you're a novice with the breed and need someone who can answer questions that pop up, it's best to purchase a dog from someone who is more knowledgeable than you are. Experienced breeders will also be more likely to raise puppies with fewer health problems.

DEDICATION: A reputable breeder is dedicated to the process of breeding Shih Tzus as close to the established breed standard as possible. In other words, they choose only the best Shih Tzus to breed from. If a breeder tells you a sire was chosen based on convenience and location alone, you should question that breeder's dedication.

OPENNESS: The best breeders are open and honest. They will tell you everything there is to know about the puppies, as well as the bloodlines from which they were bred. They will also let you meet the puppy's parents, or at a minimum, the dam. A breeder that hides information is definitely not the best breeder for you.

Reputable breeders take the business of breeding very seriously. They do genetic and health testing on the Shih Tzus they use as breeding stock to reduce the possibility of puppies carrying hereditary diseases like renal dysplasia, portal systemic shunt, allergies, immune system disorders, and inguinal hernias. Some of the other diseases your puppy's parents should have been tested for include hip dysplasia, von Willebrand's, and various thyroid disorders. If a Shih Tzu breeder isn't knowledgeable about these conditions or has no idea how to eradicate them, consider another breeder.

QUESTIONS TO ASK A BREEDER

You can never ask too many questions when choosing a breeder. Reputable and experienced breeders expect nothing less, and will probably have a few questions of their own to ask you. So don't be shy! Ask anything that comes to mind. If you're not sure where to start, here's a list of questions to keep by the phone when you begin making calls:

- How long have you been breeding Shih Tzus? *The longer the better.*

- Are you familiar with the Shih Tzu breed standard? *The answer should be yes.*

- How many breeds do you work with? *Good breeders typically only work with one or two breeds.*

- How often is the dam (the mother Shih Tzu) bred? *Responsible breeders don't breed the dam every heat cycle.*

- How did you choose the sire (the father Shih Tzu)? *Sires should be chosen based on breed standard and temperament.*

- Have genetic tests been performed on the puppies' parents? *Good breeders always have testing done, and will share the results with you if you ask for them.*

- Can I meet the parents? *You should get to see at least one of the parents.*

- Were the puppies raised in your home? *The answer should be yes.*

- Have the puppies been socialized? *Lack of socialization could lead to behavior problems.*

- Do the puppies have their shots? *Vaccinations should already be started by the time you get your puppy.*

- Have the puppies been checked for parasites? *All puppies should be tested and treated for worms.*

- How far back can you trace the puppies' bloodline? *The farther the better.*

- Am I required to spay or neuter the puppy I purchase? *It's best to know this ahead of time.*

Finally, don't forget to ask how long you'll have to wait for a puppy. Shih Tzus are popular dogs, and can sometimes be hard to come by. Many responsible breeders don't

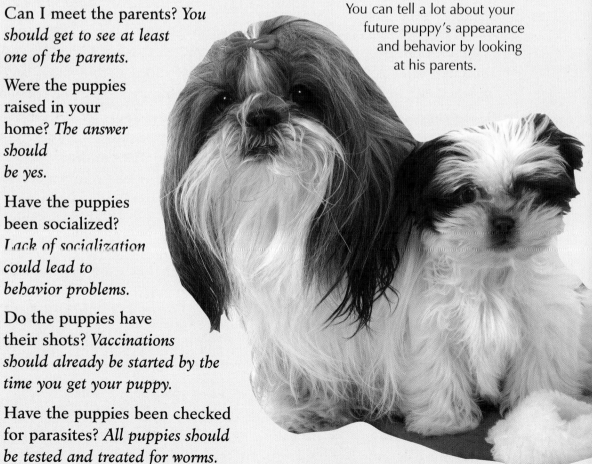

You can tell a lot about your future puppy's appearance and behavior by looking at his parents.

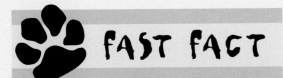

A breeder may require a 50 percent deposit if you are wait-listed. You shouldn't be alarmed at this request; it's not an unusual practice.

have puppies ready for the taking. In fact, some will not breed Shih Tzus until there is a full waiting list of owners ready to take possession of the new pups.

PAPERS THE BREEDER WILL PROVIDE

When you pick up your puppy, there are several papers your breeder should provide. The first will be a contract, which typically doubles as your bill of sale. The details and stipulations included in this document will depend on the breeder.

Most breeder's contracts stipulate that you need to take your puppy to the vet within 48 hours, and include details about the breeder's guarantee, return, and/or refund policy as well. The contract may also require you to spay or neuter your new dog within the first year, as many breeders don't sell stud or breeding rights with their puppies.

Be sure to read this document carefully before signing. The con-

tract is there to protect you, the seller, and your puppy. If there's something you don't understand, you need to ask about it. A breeder's contract is legally binding, and there will be no taking your signature off the dotted line once it's placed there.

The other papers you receive when you pick up your puppy will again depend on the breeder. At a minimum, you should receive vaccination records, pedigree papers, and the appropriate forms to register your puppy with the American Kennel Club or another appropriate registry, such as the Kennel Club of the United Kingdom, the Canadian Kennel Club, or the Field Dog Stud Book.

If you're dealing with an experienced and reputable breeder, you'll also receive papers declaring that parents of the puppy have been cleared of specific diseases. There are many different certifications, but the most important is the CERF (Canine Eye Registration

Receiving registration papers doesn't guarantee that your puppy will be healthy and well bred, but if the breeder cannot provide registration papers, you should consider another breeder.

Foundation) certification. Shih Tzus are prone to several genetic eye diseases; knowing that your puppy and his parents are free of any eye disease is very reassuring.

SHIH TZU RESCUE AND ADOPTION

If you're looking for a Shih Tzu, contacting a breeder isn't your only option. You can also turn to shelters and animal rescue organizations. Many a poor Shih Tzu has been dumped off at one of these places just because his owner got over the novelty of having a dog. Other abandoned pups may have been found running loose or may have been rescued after the death of an owner.

The chances of getting a young Shih Tzu puppy from a shelter or an animal rescue organization are slim, but there are many good dogs over the age of six months that would love nothing more than a happy home. If you were to rescue one of these dogs and give him a cherished place in your family, you can expect plenty of love, gratitude, and affection in

Rescuing or adopting an adult dog can be a rewarding experience. The dog has already gone through his puppyhood, therefore eliminating a lot of the hard work involved in raising a puppy.

return. You'll also have the satisfaction of knowing you saved a dog from a terribly lonely fate.

Of course, it should be noted that there is more to adoption than simply walking into a shelter and picking out the dog of your choice. You'll have to go through an application process. In addition to filling in basic information like your name and address, you'll be asked questions about your home (do you have kids?), your lifestyle (do you have time for a dog?), and your reasons for wanting a dog (is pet ownership just a passing fancy?).

You may also have to be willing to take on a Shih Tzu with an unknown history. Not all the dogs at shelters have papers and documented bloodlines. There is a risk that your Shih Tzu will not be purebred. There is also a chance that the dog will not be fully trained or, in a worst-case scenario, he may exhibit difficult behaviors that are tough to break.

If you do decide to adopt, please make sure you're in it for the long haul. Dogs can sometimes take a full year or longer to train. You need to be prepared to make that commitment, if necessary. Remember, the Shih Tzu you'll be taking home was already left behind once; taking the poor dog back to a shelter after you adopted him would be extremely cruel.

WHAT TO LOOK FOR IN A PUPPY

Whether you buy a Shih Tzu from a breeder or adopt a dog, you need to know what to look for in a puppy. First and foremost, you want a dog that's healthy and in good condition. Taking on a sick pup can be expensive, and may even lead to heartbreak if the animal has a serious illness that your vet cannot treat successfully.

When selecting your puppy from a breeder, he should appear happy and healthy, with bright eyes and a clean coat.

DESIGNER BREEDS

There are many crossbreeds or "designer dogs" that originate from the Shih Tzu. The American Shih Tzu Club frowns upon the practice of creating designer dogs, but there is no denying their popularity among buyers. Although breeders often use different names for Shih Tzu mixes, some of the most common terms are:

- **Shih-Poo/Shizapoo:** Cross between a Poodle and a Shih Tzu (at left)
- **Shiranian/Shihpom:** Cross between a Pomeranian and a Shih Tzu
- **Peki-Tzu:** Cross between a Pekinese and a Shih Tzu
- **Shicon/Zuchon:** Cross between a Bichon Frise and a Shih Tzu
- **Shi-wawa/ShiChi:** Cross between a Chihuahua and a Shih Tzu

While a veterinary checkup is really the only way to confirm that your pup has no physical problems, you can get a good idea of a Shih Tzu puppy's overall condition if you look the puppy over carefully yourself. To start, make sure there's no discharge from the eyes, nose, or ears. Then, check his skin and coat. Both should appear healthy and free

of parasites. The puppy's belly should be a light pink and free of rashes.

The puppy should be neither too thin nor too heavy. If his belly is swollen, it may be because it's full of worms. You should also feel the tummy to check for a hernia. Like many other breeds, Shih Tzu puppies are prone to umbilical hernias. If you feel a small lump on the tummy where the umbilical cord may have been attached, a hernia is most likely present. In some cases, this is no big deal, but a serious hernia may eventually require an operation.

JUDGING TEMPERAMENT

Just because a puppy is healthy doesn't mean that he is the right choice for you. Every puppy has a different temperament. If you don't find a Shih Tzu whose personality matches your lifestyle, you'll be sorry later on. For example, if you have children, you'll need a good-natured and energetic puppy that can hold his own in a variety of situations. On the other hand, if you have a laid-back lifestyle and no little ones, a more easygoing puppy could be the better choice.

Regardless of what you may have heard, you shouldn't let a puppy pick you. If you choose the brash puppy that runs up to you first, and isn't afraid to step on the heads of his brothers and sisters to get close to you and catch your attention, you're liable to end up with a pushy pet that's difficult to control.

At the same time, if you pick the puppy that hangs back and shows no

When evaluating a litter of puppies, take your time. Watch how each puppy reacts with the other dogs and people in the room.

interest in you, you may end up with a shy and distrustful dog that eventually turns on you or on someone else out of fear. Such dogs can be hard to bring out of their shell, and if you're a novice dog owner, the challenge may be too much to handle.

The safe bet is to choose a puppy that falls somewhere in the middle. In other words, look for a pup that is neither too dominant nor too submissive. You can get a general idea of where puppies rank on this scale by watching how they interact with you and with their littermates. If you're working with a breeder, be sure to ask about the puppies' temperaments. Often, a breeder will be able to suggest which puppy will be a good fit for you. In some cases the breeder will choose the puppy for you.

MEET THE PARENTS

Because it can be extremely difficult to tell whether or not Shih Tzu puppies have been bred to come as close as possible to the breed standard just by looking at the puppies, it's a good idea to meet the parents. You should ask to see both the dam and the sire. If the sire is not on site, the breeder may at least have a picture of him.

When you meet the puppies' relatives, take a good look at how they turned out, paying special attention to both looks and temperament. The

parents should have all the characteristics of a purebred Shih Tzu. The size of the dog, the condition of the coat, and other physical attributes should all be in line with what is considered typical for this breed.

As for temperament, both the dam and the sire should exhibit a friendly and trusting demeanor. If either of the parents is snappish, shy, or barking suspiciously, the breeder may have concentrated too much on physical conformation to the breed standard and not enough on personality. (It's also possible that the mother could just be overly protective of her puppies around strangers.) While this does not necessarily mean all the puppies in the litter will end up with the same fussy temperament, there's a chance the behavior may have been passed on and simply isn't evident yet in the puppies.

FINDING A VETERINARIAN

Before taking possession of your new Shih Tzu, you'll need to schedule an appointment with a veterinarian. The vet can examine your puppy (or adult dog) and make sure there are no obvious health problems. As mentioned earlier, most breeders will give you 48 hours to do this. If your vet does discover any problems, a reputable breeder will usually allow you to exchange or return the puppy for a full refund as long as you are within the predetermined window of time.

Because choosing a vet can be difficult, this a task that shouldn't be left to the last minute. You need to find someone who is competent, trustworthy, and familiar with the Shih Tzu breed. A good choice may be the vet your breeder uses. This vet will have already examined your puppy, and may be familiar with the parents as well.

If you don't live near the breeder or shelter, you can always get recommendations from friends, relatives, and neighbors. Pet owners are typically very willing to advise other people on which veterinarians are worth considering and which are not.

You may also want to find a vet who is a member of the American Animal Hospital Association (AAHA). The AAHA is the only exclusive companion animal veterinarian association in the United States, and is well known for establishing high standards in the veterinary profession. If your vet is a member of this association, you can be confident the vet's facility is inspected on a regular basis and meets the established standards.

Recommendations can lead you to a good vet, but there are other important factors to consider as well, such as the distance from your home to the vet's office. When you have a real emergency, precious minutes could mean the difference between life and death. In other words, having to drive an hour to get to the vet's office may not be the best thing for your pet.

You'll also need to find someone you can truly count on in an emergency. If your Shih Tzu eats a poisonous flower or gets stung by a bee on a Sunday afternoon, it's reassuring to

Veterinarians who are members of the AAHA are held to a higher standard than those who aren't members.

FAST FACT

You should take as much care finding a vet for your Shih Tzu as you would finding a doctor for a family member.

know that help is just a phone call away. Most vets and animal hospitals have a specific policy with regard to after-hour emergencies. You should ask prospective veterinarians and animal hospitals to explain their emergency policies in detail so you can make an informed decision.

MAKING A FINAL CHOICE

Once you have gathered recommendations, and considered factors like distance and off-hours emergency policies, it's time to request an interview and a tour of the facilities. If you're really lucky, you'll have two or more vets or animal hospitals to choose from. If not, hopefully you have at least one acceptable option.

A tour will give you a chance to see how clean (or unclean) a clinic is. Taking a peek around will also give you an idea of the technology the doctors use. Some vets have state-of-the-art equipment and can do everything from lab work and x-rays to laser surgery right on site. Other veterinary facilities are more limited.

During your tour, you'll meet several staff members and possibly the veterinarian as well. These personal introductions will be most helpful when it comes time to make a final decision. If the support staff provides good customer service and is kind to you, they are more likely to be kind to your pet. The same goes for the vet.

An interview will have to be scheduled at the vet's convenience. A guided tour, on the other hand, may be available at any time. To request a tour, call the facility and explain that you'll be getting a Shih Tzu and are in need of a good vet. The receptionist should be able to tell you whether or not the veterinarian is accepting new patients, and may be able to answer a few other questions. Specific things to ask about include the services that are provided on site, the experience of the staff, and payment options.

When you do get a chance to take a tour of the facilities and meet the vet, try to make the most of the experience. If necessary, make a checklist that will help you to evaluate the facility and a list of questions to ask the vet. Don't be shy; you'll be entrusting your pet's life to the clinic every time you walk in the door. As a pet owner, you have the responsibility to make sure that your Shih Tzu will be cared for properly.

CHAPTER FIVE

Caring for Your Shih Tzu Puppy (Birth to Six Months)

If you were bringing a new baby home, you would prepare a nursery as well as your family. You should do the same thing when bringing your Shih Tzu home. Shih Tzu puppies are just like small, extremely hairy babies. They depend on their owners for food and water,

It will take time for your Shih Tzu puppy to adjust to his new home. This transition will be easier for everyone if you prepare your home properly before he arrives.

as well as love, care, and guidance. It will be your responsibility to make sure your puppy is kept safe, healthy, and happy.

PUPPY-PROOFING YOUR HOME

All puppies love putting things in their mouths, and Shih Tzu puppies are no exception. The first thing your new Shih Tzu will do is explore his new surroundings. If there's a stray cord, kids' toys, or any shoes lying around, you can be sure that curiosity will lead the puppy to investigate these items with teeth and tongue as soon as the opportunity arises. That's why it's essential for you to puppy-proof your home before you pick up your puppy.

To view each room in your house as your puppy will view it, get down on your hands and knees and see what grabs your attention. Are there magazines, knickknacks, toys, or plants in reach? What about garbage cans? All these items will lure a puppy into misbehaving.

Another danger is electrical cords. Dangling cords from lamps or appliances like the television and computer are sure to draw a puppy's attention. You should make every effort to hide, tape down, or cover these cords. A puppy can be seriously injured if he manages to chew his way through the protective covering around the wire.

Consider putting child locks on kitchen or bathroom cabinets that contain cleaning supplies and other toxic products. If left alone for as little as 30 seconds, an especially curious puppy will easily be able to open cabinet doors with a nose or a paw.

Finally, don't forget about the places where only a Shih Tzu puppy could fit, such as under low tables or the bed, or behind the couch or entertainment center. For a tiny dog, these are great hiding places—and great places to soil the carpet when nobody is looking.

PUPPY-PROOFING YOUR YARD

Although Shih Tzus don't necessarily like being outside for hours on end, your pet is bound to spend some time in your backyard. That's why you need to make the same puppy-proofing efforts outside as you do inside.

Start by removing any plants, fertilizer, or lawn equipment that might be poisonous or dangerous. Next,

FAST FACT

Don't forget that Shih Tzu puppies can climb and jump. Items left on an end table or a coffee table are liable to be sniffed and possibly chewed on.

take a look around the yard to see if there's anything else that could be considered a hazard. Pools, hot tubs, hoses, and kids' toys are all good examples. An unsupervised puppy could easily fall into a pool or become trapped in the pool cover and not be able to get out, or choke on something that can be chewed into small pieces.

If you have a fenced-in yard or kennel, inspect every inch of it before letting your puppy loose. Make sure the fence is flush with the ground or

It's important to make sure your yard is safe for your Shih Tzu.

TOXIC PLANTS AND FLOWERS

If they get an opportunity, most dogs will nibble on a plant or two at some point in their life. Unfortunately, there are many plants and flowers that are toxic to dogs, and every year thousands of pets are rushed to the veterinarian after eating greenery from around the house or yard. It's a good idea to get rid of plants you know to be poisonous, or at least make sure they're out of your dog's reach.

Here's a list of some of the plants most poisonous to Shih Tzus. Keep in mind that this list is not complete. There are many other plants out there that are just as toxic, so be sure to do your research.

- Azalea
- Baby's breath
- Caladium
- Daffodil
- Elephant ears
- English ivy
- Foxglove
- Geranium
- Holly
- Hydrangea
- Lily of the valley

- Mistletoe
- Mother-in-law's tongue
- Nightshade
- Oleander
- Primrose
- Yew

For a full list of common poisonous plants, visit the Web site of the Humane Society of the United States, www.hsus.org.

buried deep in the dirt. Shih Tzu puppies are incredibly resourceful. If there's an escape route available or any way to wriggle under the fence, your puppy will find it and wander off when you're not looking.

CREATING A SECURE SPACE FOR YOUR PUPPY

Before bringing your puppy home, decide where your puppy can and cannot go. For example, if you don't want the puppy in the kids' rooms (where small toys can be ingested) or in the basement (where dangerous chemicals and tools lurk), then you need to keep the doors to these areas closed or the entryways blocked off with some sort of gate. Until your puppy learns the household rules, every place where the family goes will be considered fair game.

You should also come up with rules regarding the beds and other furniture. If you let your pet cuddle up with you in your bed or on the couch as a puppy, this behavior will surely continue as your puppy grows into adulthood. Although most Shih Tzus are eager to please, you'll undoubtedly confuse your pet by allowing a certain behavior one minute but not the next.

Even if you plan on letting your pup have the run of the house, you should still designate a place in the house to serve as a special space for your puppy while he's settling in. The space could be a laundry room or mudroom that is blocked off with a baby gate, or an exercise pen located in the kitchen, living room, or a bedroom. Anytime you leave your new puppy home alone, he should be left in this safe place.

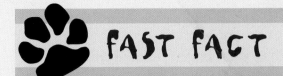

FAST FACT

Some puppies love to chew. If your puppy is chewing on wood furniture, cabinets, or other items that cannot be removed or hidden behind closed doors, try spraying Bitter Apple or another foul-tasting but nontoxic substance on the object. These products can be purchased at pet-supply stores.

Since your puppy may end up spending a significant amount of time in the space, it should be clean, comfortable, and contain everything the puppy will need (i.e., food and water dish, toys, a blanket,

Give your puppy a place in your home that he can consider his own.

etc.). To make your puppy even more comfortable, you should buy a plastic or wire crate that will serve as a sort of "bedroom" for your Shih Tzu. Dogs are den creatures and love having a space all their own. The crate should be big enough for your Shih Tzu to grow into, but not so large that the puppy can go off and urinate in a corner and not be bothered by it. In most cases, a medium-sized crate (24 to 30 inches/61 to 76 cm) will suffice for an adult Shih Tzu.

PREPARING YOUR FAMILY

Hopefully, the entire household is enthusiastic about getting a new puppy and will be willing to pitch in when needed. Of course, not everyone will know what needs to be done, so it's important to come up with some sort of game plan. Consistency will be the key to training and raising a happy, well-behaved Shih Tzu.

Sit down together and establish rules—for example, don't feed the new puppy table scraps, or don't let the puppy in the basement. If you have children, explain that your new Shih Tzu puppy is very fragile. Roughhousing or an accidental misstep could injure the puppy. Be sure to stress the importance of not leaving toys lying around the house or yard.

FAST FACT

If you can, take some time off work when you bring your new puppy home. This will give you a chance to bond with your new pal. Not having to get up early and go to work will also make those first few days (and nights) a little easier.

Many toys have small pieces, which, if swallowed, could cause your puppy to choke, become ill, or even die.

BRINGING YOUR NEW BABY HOME

The big day has finally arrived, and it's time to bring your new baby home! Before you get caught up in the excitement, make sure your puppy will have everything he needs that first night. Nothing is worse than leaving your new puppy to make a special trip to the store to pick up something you forgot.

If nothing else, you should have at least the basics: food, dishes to put food and water in, a collar, a leash, a toy or two, a crate to transport the puppy in and to use as a den, and various cleaning supplies to use when your puppy has his first "accident" on the carpet.

It's also a good idea to have a list of last-minute questions to ask the breeder or shelter. For example, you should ask about feeding times and what kind of food the puppy is eating. If you're adopting an older dog, ask whether he's paper-trained or housebroken, and what commands (if any) he is familiar with.

THE FIRST NIGHT

Your new Shih Tzu is bound to have lots of fun checking out his new pad and meeting his new family. Those first few hours will be filled with lots of sniffing, romping, and kisses. After a while, your puppy will probably succumb to exhaustion and take a little nap. If this happens, let him sleep for a bit. Chances are, he will get very little sleep once night rolls around and everyone else goes to bed.

That first night will be rough. It will probably be the first time your puppy has ever been away from his dam and littermates overnight. As you can imagine, this is a very traumatic experience. Your puppy will let you know it, too, by crying and whining his heart out. As tempting as it will be to go check on him over and over again to try and comfort him, you need to restrain yourself. Give in repeatedly to his whining throughout the night, and he will do it every single night just to get your attention.

If you want to make things easier on your puppy, and reassure him, put his crate in your bedroom. Sometimes just being able to see someone else is all a puppy needs to settle down and fall asleep. You can also put a hot water bottle or a piece of bedding from his former home in the crate to offer warmth or the comforting scent of something familiar.

THE FIRST FEW MONTHS

The first few months of Shih Tzu ownership will be a whirlwind. Your puppy will seem to be growing bigger and getting bolder by the day. During this time, he will become more and more accustomed to his new surroundings. Your puppy will also be very impressionable at this stage in his life, so it's important to give him lots of love and attention.

It's also essential for you to develop routines for him at this time. Your puppy should have a regular feeding schedule and should be taken outside frequently so that he gets in the habit of eliminating in other places besides on newspaper or the Oriental rug. However, you shouldn't expect too much at this stage—it takes time for a puppy to develop cognitive skills and learn all the rules associated with a particular household.

How far along your puppy is at this point will most likely depend on how old he was when you brought

Establish daily routines for your puppy. He wants and needs your direction.

him home. Some breeders will let Shih Tzus go at eight weeks, but most of them follow the recommendation of the American Shih Tzu Club, which is 12 weeks.

When Shih Tzus are 12 to 16 weeks old, they are in what is considered to be the "terrible twos" stage for dogs. Puppies of this age are curious, demanding of time and attention, and above all, willful. Getting your puppy to do his business outside and follow other household rules will be a daily battle. His behavior will often be confusing and frustrating. The best thing you can do is work through it.

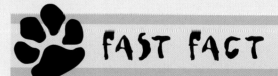

FAST FACT

Between three and sixteen weeks of age, your puppy will experience what is known as a fear period. Fright and pain should be avoided at all costs. Too many negative incidents during this period could turn your Shih Tzu into a fearful or aggressive dog.

Shih Tzus love to please their owners. If you're consistent in your training during this time and over the next few months, give your puppy plenty of praise when he does the right things, and guide him patiently in the direction you need him to go when he misbehaves, you'll eventually end up with a well-trained dog.

FIRST TRIP TO THE VET

Since you scheduled an appointment with a veterinarian prior to picking up your pup, you should have no problems getting your new Shih Tzu examined within the first 24 to 48 hours of ownership.

Chances are this will not be the puppy's first or even second visit to a veterinarian. For this reason, your puppy may not be that excited about getting poked and prodded by his new doctor. Still, you should do your best to make sure the experience is a positive one.

Be sure to bring along all required materials, such as your puppy's vaccination record, pedigree papers, and any other documents the breeder gave you. The vet will be able to make copies of this information and evaluate your new pet's history.

If your puppy has defecated between the time you picked him up and the trip to the vet, you should collect the stool in a plastic bag and take it with you. The vet will be able to check the stool sample for parasites.

THE PHYSICAL EXAM AND SOCIALIZATION CHECKUP

Your puppy's first visit to the vet will consist of a full physical exam and socialization checkup. The exact order of things will vary depending on the vet's office, but most physical exams start with a weigh-in and a temperature check. Hopefully, the puppy is neither underweight nor overweight, and has a temperature of 100° to 102.5° Fahrenheit (37.8° to 39.1° Celsius).

The vet will then look over the puppy's ears, eyes, nose, teeth, gums, and genitals before moving on to the skin and coat. Things the vet will be checking for include a hernia, discharge, signs of infection, and parasites. A good vet will also listen carefully to the puppy's heartbeat and check other internal organs by massaging different parts of the puppy's body.

Throughout the exam, the vet will keep you updated, and may even talk to you about some of the illnesses that most commonly affect Shih Tzu puppies, such as kennel cough, pneumonia, and other upper respiratory disorders. If your Shih Tzu is older, your vet will discuss genetic disorders affecting adult dogs, like renal (kidney) failure, skin problems, and joint issues.

Before the physical exam is over, you may want to ask the vet to give you an assessment of your puppy's personality. With a few simple tests, the vet will be able to tell whether your puppy is dominant, submissive, independent, or normal by nature. This assessment will either confirm the fact that you made the right choice or give you something to worry about. In any case, it will be helpful when it comes time to train your puppy. It will also allow you to better guess how your new friend may react to various social interactions.

LAB TESTS

If you managed to obtain a stool sample from your puppy, the vet will use it to perform a fecal examination. This examination is important to determine whether or not your Shih Tzu has worms. If worms are present, the vet will begin de-worming treatment immediately.

There are several other lab tests that can be performed on your puppy. The tests will often depend on the vet, as well as the information that has been obtained from the breeder or animal shelter. Shih Tzus are prone to a bleeding disorder known as von Willebrand's disease.

Since puppies as young as seven to eight weeks old can be tested for this disorder, the breeder may have already taken care of this.

A cheek swab can also be performed on your puppy to test for renal dysplasia, a kidney disease that is common among Shih Tzus. The first stage of this disease has been known to strike—and in some cases, cause renal failure in—puppies. The swab can be taken in the vet's office, but usually must be sent out for analysis.

VACCINATIONS

Your puppy will need several vaccines (puppy inoculations) to protect him from serious and sometimes fatal illnesses. These vaccinations will continue throughout his life and will often be referred to as booster shots later on. The diseases and viruses your Shih Tzu should be protected from include the following:

DISTEMPER: Distemper is a highly contagious and dangerous virus that can be transmitted through the air and through contact with fecal matter. It's virtually incurable, and frequently fatal to Shih Tzus. Infected dogs that are able to recover are typically left paralyzed or partially paralyzed, and often suffer irreparable damage to the nervous system. Initial symptoms of canine distemper include vomiting, diarrhea, runny nose and eyes, coughing, and a poor appetite. Puppies are especially vulnerable to distemper and must be vaccinated at the earliest opportunity.

HEPATITIS: Also known as canine adenovirus (CAV), infectious canine hepatitis is a contagious disease of the liver. Infected dogs, wolves, coyotes, and bears transmit the disease through feces, urine, blood, saliva, or eye and nasal discharge. CAV attacks the liver and the kidneys, and may cause bleeding disorders or even death. Shih Tzus that do recover from this disease often have permanent kidney and liver conditions. Initial symptoms of canine hepatitis are fever, depression, coughing, poor appetite, vomiting, and diarrhea.

LEPTOSPIROSIS: Leptospirosis is a bacterial disease that affects dogs, humans, and other animals. Infected animals transmit the disease through blood or urine, which can contaminate

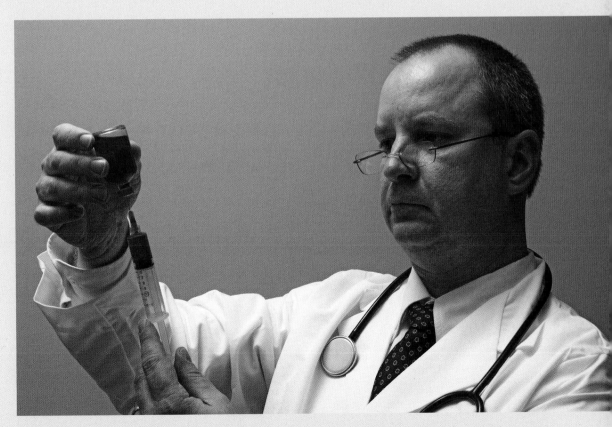

Your Shih Tzu's first visit to the veterinarian will be very important. Your dog will be evaluated and tested for potential physical problems as well as vaccinated against various diseases.

VACCINATION SCHEDULE

Here is a typical Shih Tzu puppy vaccination schedule:

Six to Eight Weeks Old: First distemper, hepatitis, leptospirosis, parainfluenza, parvovirus shot. This is typically given in one combined injection, known as the DHLPP shot or simply as the distemper shot.

10 to 12 Weeks Old: Second distemper, hepatitis, leptospirosis, parainfluenza, parvovirus (DHLPP) shot. Again, given in one combined injection.

14 to 16 Weeks Old: Third and final distemper, hepatitis, leptospirosis, parainfluenza, parvovirus (DHLPP) shot. Again, given in one combined injection.

Four to Six Months Old: Rabies shot. This shot can be given to puppies as young as 12 weeks of age, but some states don't recognize rabies vaccinations given before the puppy is 16 weeks old. For clarification, ask your vet about the laws in your state.

Your puppy may or may not need three other vaccines, depending on your location and lifestyle. The first is the bordetella (kennel cough) vaccine, which is generally given to puppies that will be spending time with other dogs at a boarder, groomer, or training class. Bordetella causes a dry, hacking cough that sounds as though your dog needs to clear his throat, but it recurs all day long and can be very annoying for both you and your Shih Tzu. This shot can be given as early as five weeks, and is highly recommended for Shih Tzus that will not be trained and groomed at home.

The second optional vaccination is intended to protect puppies from Lyme disease, which is passed on by deer ticks and can cause lameness, lethargy, and kidney problems. This vaccination is somewhat controversial because it is known to occasionally interfere with a dog's immune system. Unless you live in a high-risk area, your vet may advise against the Lyme disease inoculation.

The third and final vaccination may be optional, depending on your vet. This vaccine protects against coronavirus, a disease that causes a variety of health problems but usually is not life-threatening. In rare cases, the disease can be fatal. Some vets include the coronavirus vaccine in the DHLPP shots; others do not. Those who do offer this vaccination will usually refer to the injection as a DHLPPC shot.

soil and water. Recovered animals can also be carriers, and may continue to transmit the disease for months or even years. The disease is treatable if caught early enough; however, irreparable damage may be done to the organs. The earliest symptoms of leptospirosis include fever, vomiting, diarrhea, poor appetite, stiffness, jaundice, internal bleeding, and lethargy. Some puppies may not exhibit any symptoms, which makes this disease particularly dangerous.

PARAINFLUENZA: Parainfluenza is an extremely contagious respiratory virus. It's most frequently transmitted through nasal secretions and can cause mild respiratory infections. In Shih Tzu puppies, this often leads to pneumonia, which will make a puppy very sick. If left untreated, it can be fatal. Symptoms of parainfluenza include a fever, loss of appetite, and a dry, hacking cough.

PARVOVIRUS: Also known simply as parvo, canine parvovirus is a contagious viral disease that is typically transmitted through fecal matter. The virus can live for up to one year in the soil, and up to ten days on shoes, paws, and hair. While the disease is manageable if caught early enough, it is fatal 50 percent of the time. Most deaths occur 24 to 72 hours after symptoms appear. The symptoms include severe vomiting, bloody diarrhea, and a high fever. All puppies are extremely susceptible to parvovirus, but some longhaired breeds, like Shih Tzus, are much more vulnerable than other breeds. Keep your puppy away from other dogs and avoid walks to the park until all his parvovirus inoculations are complete.

RABIES: Rabies is a viral disease that attacks the brain. Infected wildlife can transmit this disease to dogs through saliva. Humans can also contract this disease. Rabies is almost always fatal to dogs, and is nearly always fatal to humans if left untreated. Symptoms of rabies include aggressiveness, foaming at the mouth, and paralysis. Most state laws require dogs to be vaccinated. Your vet will be able to tell you how soon your Shih Tzu puppy can

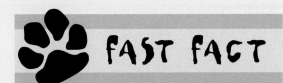

FAST FACT

Like puppies of other breeds, Shih Tzu puppies can carry worms that infect other pets as well as people. Children are especially vulnerable. Your puppy must be tested—and, if necessary, treated—for worms as soon as possible.

receive this inoculation—typically, between the 16th and 26th weeks of life.

Not every veterinarian has the same vaccination protocol. Some vets begin to administer puppy inoculations when the puppy is eight weeks old; others begin as early as five or six weeks of age. According to the American Kennel Club, vaccinations should begin at five or six weeks of age and continue periodically for several weeks, with the puppy receiving all inoculations required for the first year (except the rabies shot), by the time he is 16 weeks old.

Since vaccinations will most likely be started by the time you get your puppy from the breeder or shelter, you should stick to whatever schedule has already been established. This will protect your pup from any serious illnesses, and ensure immunity after maternal antibodies have disappeared.

PUPPY NUTRITION

Nursing Shih Tzu puppies receive nourishment and important antibodies from their mother for the first six weeks of their lives. On occasion, there will be one puppy that doesn't get to nurse quite as much as his littermates. When this happens, the breeder takes charge and feeds the puppy by bottle. If the puppy is really tiny, an eyedropper is sometimes used.

Nursing puppies usually feed every two hours for the first three weeks. During this time, they will get bigger and bigger, gaining weight on a daily basis. When the puppies are three to four weeks of age, the breeder begins the weaning process. Puppies are still allowed to nurse, but they are also given a gruel-like mixture of ground kibble, water, and milk substitute. Some breeders start alternating milk and meat meals at this time. As each week passes, the breeder mixes in more kibble and makes less of an effort to grind it up. By the time puppies are eight weeks old, they are generally fully weaned and eating puppy food exclusively.

THE PROPER DIET FOR YOUR PUPPY

Weaned puppies should receive a diet of quality dry kibble. Canned food, although palatable, contains too much water, and is generally not as effective when it comes to controlling plaque and tartar on your pet's teeth. Dry kibble is the preferred choice for Shih Tzus.

When you pick up your puppy from the breeder or shelter, you'll probably be given a bag of food to take with you, or at least a recommendation as to what you should feed the puppy. If you don't keep the puppy on the same diet he's used to, or don't feed him at his regularly scheduled times, he will almost certainly get an upset tummy.

After a few days, you can gradually introduce a different brand of food into your Shih Tzu's diet. Whatever brand you pick, be sure to check the label on the package. If it does not include the American Association of Feed Control Officials (AAFCO) stamp of approval, then the food almost certainly does not contain the appropriate amount of vitamins and minerals for your pet. You'll also want to take a close look at the ingredient list. Animal proteins should be the number-one ingredient. Foods that have a grain or corn base are not as good for your puppy's health. Puppies need protein and fatty acids for energy and to build muscles and connective tissue.

If you're still in doubt, speak to your veterinarian. A good vet will be able to recommend several different brands that would be good for your Shih Tzu, and will also be able to advise you on the best feeding schedule as your puppy grows.

SOCIALIZATION

The most critical socialization period for your Shih Tzu is during the first twelve weeks of his life. This is when Shih Tzu puppies form their impression of the world around them. Human contact is of utmost importance, as is contact with other animals.

Socialization often begins at the breeder's, when a puppy is five or six weeks old, but it must be continued after you bring your puppy home. If a pup is not exposed to other people and animals, or experiences like

Introduce your Shih Tzu to all of the people in your home as soon as possible.

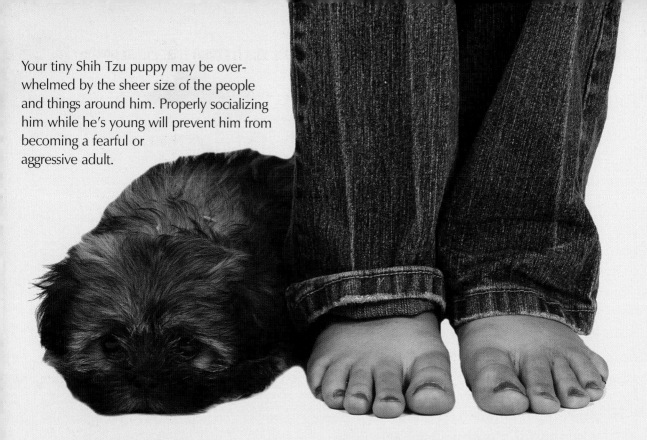

Your tiny Shih Tzu puppy may be overwhelmed by the sheer size of the people and things around him. Properly socializing him while he's young will prevent him from becoming a fearful or aggressive adult.

riding in a car or getting groomed, it will be very frightening for him to encounter these things later in life.

You should start the socialization process as soon as you bring your Shih Tzu puppy home. Introduce him to everyone in the household, and then take him out to meet other people. The more human contact and affection he is exposed to, the better.

Of course, be sure your puppy has all his necessary vaccinations before walking him anywhere on a leash. You never know what parasite, virus, or bacteria he might pick up from a grubby street or even from a neighbor's lawn. You should also carefully supervise your pup's interactions with other people. A negative

experience during the first eight months could make your pup feel uncomfortable around people or other animals. This sense of discomfort in social situations could manifest itself in fear, aggressiveness, or shyness later in your dog's life.

PUPPY SOCIALS

Once your puppy has received all his vaccinations, it's time to introduce him to other animals. If your neighbors, friends, or family members have dogs, consider inviting them over for a puppy social. However, be careful when choosing what type of dogs your Shih Tzu puppy is around. You don't want your pup to be forced to interact with an aggressive dog, especially a large one. This could create a negative experience for everyone involved.

If you're nervous about choosing a pal for your pooch, you could instead opt for socialization in a more formal setting. There are many puppy socialization programs that are administered by trainers, breeders, behavior consultants, and pet societies. These programs are sometimes called puppy socialization classes or puppy kindergarten.

In a class, puppies are introduced to one another in a safe setting. They get to rub noses, share toys, and learn basic social etiquette. There is generally lots of romping and playing, and everyone gets to have a good time—dog owners included. By the time the program ends, all the puppies will have some new friends, and most importantly, will know how to approach and interact with other dogs in the future.

Puppy socialization classes can be very good for a puppy. They can also be good for owners who like to swap stories and show off their babies. It's essential, however, for you to choose the right class. Each one is run a little differently, depending on who's in charge. To make sure that you find the right class for you and your puppy, you should do a little research ahead of time, and, if possible, get recommendations or references.

SOCIALIZATION TIPS

If you're inexperienced with puppy socialization, here are a few tips that will help guide you through the process:

- Don't overwhelm your puppy the moment you bring him home. He should be introduced to new people and new experiences gradually.

- Do your best to make every social experience a positive one.

- Always be gentle and affectionate. It's important for your Shih Tzu puppy to receive lots of love and handling during this critical period.

- Pain and fright should be avoided for the first 16 weeks. Instead of disciplining your puppy when he does something wrong, praise him when he does something right.

- Try to introduce your puppy to a new experience every day. Get him used to car rides, the vacuum, walks in the park, trips to the vet, stairs, the blender, grooming, the television, and outside noises, to name a few examples.

- If your puppy does exhibit fear, don't coddle him. This will only encourage fearful behavior. At the same time, don't force a puppy to approach something that scares him. It could make the fear worse.

- Ask people to squat, sit, or kneel to get down to Shih Tzu level. This will make interactions less intimidating for your puppy.

- Before introducing your puppy to an excited child, be sure to explain how important it is to be gentle and nice to the puppy. An overzealous child can easily hurt a tiny Shih Tzu by handling him too roughly.

- If you're unsure about what to do, talk to your breeder and veterinarian. They will have a lot of great tips and tricks you can implement.

GROOMING

If you want your Shih Tzu to have a long and beautiful coat, you need to make a point of brushing out his hair on a daily basis. Otherwise, your sweet little pooch will suffer the pain that comes with dematting a straggly coat.

You should introduce your Shih Tzu puppy to the process of grooming early.

You can start by taking just a few moments each day to brush his hair. This will get your puppy used to the idea, and allow you to gradually increase the duration of each session without a whole lot of fuss. Be forewarned, though; not every Shih Tzu puppy will be thrilled with the prospect of being groomed. In fact, most would rather play with a squeaky toy or sit in the window than get brushed. You are going to have to be firm, yet gentle. If you give in to every whimper or escape attempt, you'll end up with a dog

Keeping your Shih Tzu's coat knot-free takes daily brushing.

that is a nightmare to groom. Be persistent and kind, and do your best to make every grooming session a pleasant experience. Your Shih Tzu will eventually learn to enjoy the special time that you spend together—even if it means getting bathed, blow-dried, and brushed.

At a minimum, a Shih Tzu needs to have his entire coat brushed every other day. You'll also need to style the hair on the head into a topknot, and clean and dry the hair on the face on a daily basis.

If you're not prepared to dedicate the time and effort required to keeping your puppy's coat long, you should seriously consider a puppy cut (also called a pet trim) instead. Your Shih Tzu will still look as cute as ever, and you'll both be happier. Puppy cuts can be given after your Shih Tzu is four to six months of age. You'll have to take your pet to a groomer every four to six weeks to keep his hair properly trimmed. You'll still need to brush the hair on at least a weekly basis, but the style will be much easier to maintain than the traditional Shih Tzu cut.

BRUSHING TECHNIQUES

If you get your puppy used to standing and lying down on a grooming table, daily brushing sessions will be much more pleasant for both of you. It should be relatively easy to get your Shih Tzu to stand on the table. If you're having a problem, there are many different arms, harnesses, and other gadgets you can buy at pet stores to ease the process.

Getting your puppy to roll over and lie on his side may take a bit more effort. Chances are he will resist initially. You can trick him into staying put by rolling him over and rubbing his tummy until he's docile and happy. Then, you can start brushing. After a few brushstrokes, follow with some more tummy rubbing. Eventually, your puppy will associate the experience of lying down on the grooming table with love and attention.

If you don't have a table, you can try laying the puppy on the floor or in your lap. For some Shih Tzus, this technique works better and keeps them calmer. Of course, there are more opportunities for escape this way, so you have to keep a firm hold on your puppy the entire time.

Regardless of how you decide to position your puppy, you should start brushing at the bottom and work your way up to the top. You can move from the feet to the legs to the belly—remember to be especially gentle here with a female Shih Tzu, because of her nipples—and eventually to the top center of the back. To make the hair easier to groom, some Shih Tzu owners choose to lightly mist the coat with a pint-sized spray bottle that contains a teaspoon of conditioner mixed with water. This makes the hair easier to tame and prevents breakage or split ends.

Always brush gently with a pin brush, and always brush just one layer at a time, making sure you get every hair from skin to tip. If you encounter a large or particularly stubborn mat, don't tug, rip, or run for the scissors. Instead, saturate the mat with cream rinse or a detangling solution, then try to gently break it apart with your fingers or a special dematting tool.

Most mats appear behind the ears, where the hair is especially thick; in the armpits; and on the legs. Be sure to check these spots carefully. You may also want to finish the job with a steel comb to make sure you didn't miss any snarls or matted pieces of hair.

TOPKNOTS

Shih Tzus have very sensitive eyes, so you must keep the facial hair above their nose and between their eyes tied back in what is called a topknot. To create a topknot, simply part the hair between the eyes with a comb, and tie it up with an elastic band. Many owners use dental elastics or latex bands because they are cheap, easy to cut out, and don't break the hair.

You can pouf the front of the topknot and anchor it securely to the skull by taking a few hairs from the banded section and pulling them gently. Be careful not to pull the hair

Your Shih Tzu will be happier when his long hair is kept out of his eyes with a good topknot.

Without a topknot, your Shih Tzu will find the long hair in his eyes annoying (left). An alternative to the topknot is to have the hair around your dog's face clipped short (above).

too tightly, as this will tug on the eyes and cause your Shih Tzu discomfort. If done well, the topknot should stay put for a significant period of time, but it will probably need to be retied on a daily basis.

At four or five months old, your puppy should have enough hair to pin up. If you don't want to take the time to keep the topknot up, cutting off the facial hair at four months of age is recommended. Although a topknot is a must for Shih Tzu in the show ring, dogs that have a puppy cut can have the hair on their head cut short as well.

BATHING

At some point, you'll need to give your puppy a bath. Some owners, especially those who show Shih Tzus, bathe their pets as often as once a week. Although Shih Tzus are vain little dogs, such frequent bathing isn't necessary to keep the coat in good condition.

No matter how often you decide to bathe your Shih Tzu, you should try to make the experience as pleasant as possible. To start, make sure you set aside a nice chunk of time to get the job done. It takes a while to wash all that hair. You also need to find a place that's comfortable for both of you. Because Shih Tzus are so small, many owners choose to bathe their pet in a laundry tub or even the kitchen sink. Regardless of where you do it, you'll most definitely need a hose or spray attachment to rinse out the shampoo.

After testing the water to make sure it's neither too hot nor too cold (the water should be lukewarm), wet the dog down. Be very careful not to get any water in his ears, eyes, or up his nose. Water in the nose and eyes is uncomfortable, and water in the ears can cause an infection. Protect your pup's ears from getting wet by placing cotton balls in the ears before you begin his bath.

Once the hair is thoroughly wet, you can start working in the shampoo. Try not to tangle the hair as you do this. Remember, Shih Tzu hair is similar to human hair, so work the suds in the same way you would if you were washing your own hair. Again, be very careful not to get any water or shampoo in the dog's eyes.

If your Shih Tzu's hair is really dirty or if it has been a while since his last bath, you may want to shampoo and rinse, then repeat. You can then follow up with a conditioner that will detangle the coat and soothe the skin, and a good rinse to remove any lingering residue.

DRYING

Your Shih Tzu needs to be dried and brushed immediately after his bath. If left to air dry, his coat will end up wavy and hopelessly tangled. You can save yourself drying time by squeezing excess water out of the coat, and then bundling your pet in a towel. Make sure to use a large and very absorbent bath towel, though, or you'll be the one who looks like you just bathed!

After most of the water has been squeezed out or soaked up, you can thoroughly dry your Shih Tzu with a blow dryer. The dryer can be set on

FAST FACT

Always, always, always brush your Shih Tzu before giving him a bath. This point cannot be stressed enough. Mats in the hair become hard as cement when they're wet, which means they're almost impossible to remove after your pet's bath.

warm, but should not be too hot. You can test the heat level with your own arm—when you're satisfied with the setting, start drying at the top and brush the hair as you go. Pay special attention to the hair on the back of the neck and behind the ears. This thick hair usually takes the longest to dry.

DENTAL CARE

You wouldn't go without brushing your teeth or visiting your dentist for regular cleanings, and neither should your Shih Tzu. From the time your puppy is six months old, plaque will begin to develop and build up on his permanent teeth. Brushing with a specially formulated doggie toothpaste and toothbrush will remove the bulk of the buildup and keep your pet's teeth and gums healthy.

Eating kibble can help keep your Shih Tzu's teeth clean. When he chews the hard kibble, the pieces scrape plaque and tartar from the enamel. There are also several chew toys and products on the market that are good for your puppy's teeth. Your veterinarian will be able to recommend one or more products that will be good for your Shih Tzu's teeth.

After brushing your dog's teeth and buying chew toys, the best thing you can do for your Shih Tzu is have his teeth examined by a vet at least

Shih Tzus are more likely to develop dental problems than some larger dog breeds. To prevent these problems, get into the habit of checking and cleaning your Shih Tzu's teeth regularly.

once each year. The vet can check for early signs of periodontal disease, which is extremely common in adult Shih Tzus, and in some cases can be fatal. If necessary, the vet can also perform a prophylactic cleaning to scale and polish the teeth. This is done under anesthesia.

NAIL CARE

Trimming your pet's nails is a necessary part of the grooming routine. Some Shih Tzus need their nails trimmed every two or three weeks; others can be clipped less frequently. You can either trim your puppy's nails at home or you can take him to a vet or a pet groomer to have this done. Either way, get your puppy used to nail clipping as soon as possible. This will make the experience much more pleasant for both of you.

If you plan to do the job yourself, you'll need nail clippers specially made for dogs. You should also have a styptic pencil, styptic powder, or another clotting agent on hand. If you cut the dog's nail too short, it will bleed profusely until a clotting agent has been applied.

Hold your dog steady, and search for the quick of the nail before trimming. The quick runs through the center of the nail. On dark or black nails, the quick is hard to see, but it must be avoided. If you can't see the quick,

you need to proceed carefully, and clip off only the very tip of each nail.

Be sure to talk to your dog in a soothing voice throughout this procedure. If you can put your puppy at ease, he will not squirm or try to run away.

RECOMMENDED GROOMING SCHEDULE

Establishing and sticking to a regular grooming schedule will keep your Shih Tzu healthy and looking good. Here are recommendations that you should follow when developing his grooming schedule:

DAILY: Brush your Shih Tzu every day, or, at a minimum, every other day. Use a pin brush to groom and a steel comb to check for mats. Clean his face, redo his topknot, and check his eyes for any signs of irritation or infection. If necessary, clean and trim the hair around the anus.

TWICE WEEKLY: By five months of age, your puppy will have his permanent teeth. You should brush his teeth at least twice each week to combat plaque buildup. Also check for sores, swollen gums, or misaligned teeth.

WEEKLY: Use ear powder and hair clippers or tweezers to remove excess ear hair. Clean the ears with a cotton ball and a veterinarian-recommended cleaner or a 50/50 mixture of vinegar and water. If you notice an unusual odor coming from the ears, contact the vet immediately.

MONTHLY: Bathe your Shih Tzu, clip his nails, and, if necessary, take him to the groomer for a trim. At a minimum, clip the hair from the pads of his feet.

If your Shih Tzu is a show dog, grooming is serious business. A Shih Tzu's long, glorious coat distinguishes this breed in the ring. For this reason, it's a good idea to take your show dog to a professional groomer to keep him looking his very best.

TRAINING

Training your Shih Tzu is an ongoing process. The first year and a half is an especially trying time. You'll not only have to housebreak your puppy, but also teach him manners and general household rules.

Some inexperienced owners choose to take their dogs to a professional trainer or obedience school. This isn't a bad idea, but it's not absolutely necessary, either. With a little bit of patience, hard work, and a few good tips, you can mold your puppy into the dog you want him to be.

To start, you need to teach your puppy which behaviors are acceptable and which are not. Two behaviors that should be nipped in the bud right away include jumping up on people and biting.

Although Shih Tzus are small, they can hurt themselves or someone else if they jump up to greet every guest who walks through the door. You need to curb this behavior early by placing the puppy's feet back on the ground and making him stand every time a guest enters. Give him praise when he does this correctly. This will demonstrate the behavior you expect.

Biting should also be addressed early. It's normal for a puppy to bite and chew when playing with his littermates, and it's normal for him to try this with humans as well. The problem is that human skin isn't quite as tough as puppy skin. To get your puppy to stop biting, you should say "Ouch" or make a noise that will startle him every time he bites. Then, ignore the puppy for a moment. When you start playing with him again, praise him as long as he's not biting. If he bites, startle him and ignore him again. Eventually, he will get the message that biting is unacceptable.

The key is consistency. If you're consistent in teaching your Shih Tzu

You can begin training your Shih Tzu to stay before you teach him to sit, but it's usually better to do it the other way around. Puppies are typically calmer and less apt to stray when they're in a sitting position.

the rules, he'll be eager to please and learn quickly. If, on the other hand, you constantly change commands or let him get away with a certain behavior one minute and not the next, your puppy will be confused and unresponsive to your training methods.

It's also important to be kind, patient, and gentle. You should never physically hit your puppy when trying to correct a behavior. The best way to get a pup to stop doing something is to direct him to the correct behavior and praise him when he acts appropriately.

TEACHING BASIC COMMANDS

There are several basic commands you should teach your puppy before he's six months old: sit, down, stay, and come. It's almost never too early to begin. In fact, the sooner you start, the better. Just remember to keep the training sessions short and

fun. Puppies have limited attention spans, and will become bored and willful if training goes on too long.

SIT: Teaching your puppy to sit is one of the easiest ways to control his behavior. To start, get the puppy's attention with a small treat held in your hand. Hold the treat above his nose and tell him to sit. Make sure he has to reach up to get it, but does not have to jump. He should fall naturally into the sitting position. If not, you can very gently push down on his haunches (his rear end, right below the spine and between the hip joints.) When he sits down, praise him enthusiastically and give him a bit of the treat. Repeat this exercise for two minutes straight, three to four times a day.

DOWN: Once your dog has mastered the sit command, you can build on this knowledge to teach him to lie down on command. Once again, you'll use a treat to encourage the

The down command is a great way to calm your Shih Tzu, or to keep him from getting in the way while you tend to a problem elsewhere in the house.

Training your Shih Tzu to sit and lay down takes time and practice. However, for his own safety your dog must master these commands.

appropriate response. Start by getting your Shih Tzu into a sitting position. Hold the treat in front of him, at nose level, then give the command, "Down." It may help to use his name first, to make sure you have his attention. At the same time, move the treat down and away from his face. Your Shih Tzu should lean forward and follow the treat down. Once his belly touches the ground, reward him with praise and the treat. Practice this exercise for two minutes, three or four times a day.

STAY/COME: The stay and come commands go hand in hand, which means you can teach your puppy to stay and come simultaneously. Begin by getting your Shih Tzu to sit. Then, holding your hand up like a stop sign, give the command, "Stay." Be sure to say it in a firm voice. If your puppy remains in the sitting position, give him lots of praise. Repeat the exercise, only this time, back away slowly as you issue the stay command. When you get a step or two away from your pup, tell him to come. You can use a treat for extra encouragement. Repeat both the stay and come portion of the exercise for at least two minutes straight, three to four times a day, gradually increasing the distance between you and your pup.

HOUSEBREAKING

Housebreaking a Shih Tzu puppy can be a challenge. It often takes a minimum of six months for a puppy to get into a routine and get full control over his bladder. Until then, there will be accidents—lots and lots of accidents. It's best to accept this ahead of time, since there is really nothing you can do about it. Accidents are just part of raising a puppy.

A Shih Tzu puppy's bladder is incredibly small. No matter how hard a puppy tries to hold his urine, he will only be able to last an hour or two during the first 12 weeks. After that, he acquires a bit more control. Nevertheless, he will need to relieve himself every four hours, on average.

The need to eliminate usually occurs when the puppy first wakes up, after eating, and following playtime. Always taking your Shih Tzu outside at these key times will encourage good behavior. So he knows what's expected, you should take him to the same spot in the yard every time and issue a command, such as "Go potty."

If you're not available to let the puppy out at these designated times or throughout the day as needed, you must hire a pet sitter or prevail on a neighbor to do the job for you. Pets that eliminate on the carpet or floor throughout the day don't understand why they cannot keep this behavior up at night.

When your puppy does his business in the designated area, always shower him with praise. This will let him know that you approve. You can also give him a small treat for extra reinforcement.

If your puppy has an accident and makes a mess in the house, don't punish him. Rubbing his nose in his own urine will not teach him to go outside. It will, however, teach him that you are mean and not to be

trusted. Simply clean up the mess, move on, and remember to take your dog out more frequently.

HOUSEBREAKING TECHNIQUES

You can train your Shih Tzu to relieve himself outside or somewhere in the house on paper. Every owner has a preferred method. Whichever you choose, you should probably

Try not to lose your temper when your puppy has an accident. Getting angry or upset won't accomplish anything. Accidents are to be expected, as they are part of the learning process.

stick with it. It's confusing for puppies to be trained outside for months, and then be expected to eliminate on papers inside.

Also, don't give your Shih Tzu full run of the house when you aren't around. Instead, confine him to a small area, like the utility room or the kitchen, while you're away. This will prevent him from making unnoticed messes on the carpet. If he's being paper-trained, be sure to include his papers in this area.

Many owners use crates to confine their puppies. You may think this is cruel, but it's not. Shih Tzus are den animals by nature; they love having a place to call their own. A crate usually becomes a puppy's home inside the home. As long as the crate is a proper size, this is a good way to confine your pet while you're away.

As your puppy gets greater control of his bladder, you can also use the crate as a housebreaking tool while you're away. Most puppies don't like to relieve themselves where they sleep, although they will

do so if they're forced to. Never leave a puppy confined to a crate for more than two to four hours.

ESTABLISHING HOUSEHOLD RULES

Puppies can develop many bad behaviors, such as jumping on strangers, barking, chewing on furniture, or biting. It's up to you to make sure these behaviors are corrected and eliminated before they become ingrained habits.

Make the rules very clear for your puppy. You'll gain the puppy's respect by making him follow rules consistently. Being too permissive with your puppy is a recipe for disaster. If you give a Shih Tzu puppy an inch, he'll take a mile. You must teach him who's boss.

There are several ways to establish yourself as the pack leader. First, control when and how your puppy eats. Make him sit before you put the dish down. Every once in a while, you should also take the food from his mouth or remove the dish before he's finished. This will let him know that he's not in charge of his food consumption and discourage him from getting snarly if people are around when he eats.

Second, make him walk properly. When he's on a leash, he should follow your lead rather than pulling you in any direction he wants to go.

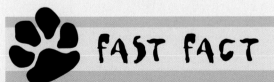

FAST FACT

Don't ever force your puppy into a crate. It will scare him. Instead, coax him inside with toys or some of his favorite treats.

If you don't want your Shih Tzu lounging on the furniture, be firm and always enforce the rules. Eventually, he will learn his boundaries.

Remember to lead him gently, though. If you yank him around, he'll be afraid he's going to be hurt every time you put the leash on.

Finally, make your Shih Tzu mind his manners. He should not jump on visitors when they come over, bark to get his way, play too roughly, or bite anyone's fingers. If he's allowed to get away with this kind of behavior once or twice, he won't understand that he's doing anything wrong the third, fourth, or fifth time.

COGNITIVE DEVELOPMENT

The cognitive development schedule shown here offers an indication of what you can expect from your puppy in the first six months. Keep in mind that every Shih Tzu is different. Your puppy may reach maturity faster or slower than average.

BIRTH TO TWO WEEKS: At this age, a puppy can do very little for himself, and needs his mother for food and warmth. Sleep is about the only other thing on a puppy's mind, although he will respond to gentle touching.

TWO TO SEVEN WEEKS: In this short period, puppies develop their motor skills, vision, and hearing. They also begin to interact more with their mother and littermates, and learn how to function within a pack.

EIGHT TO TWELVE WEEKS: By eight weeks of age, a Shih Tzu puppy's brain is fully developed. At this time, the puppy should be socializing more with humans than with his canine pack, and learning about the world around him.

THIRTEEN TO SIXTEEN WEEKS: At this time, the puppy has moved into an adolescent stage, and acts like it. He tests every boundary imaginable. He will also begin to associate praise and punishment with certain behaviors.

SEVENTEEN WEEKS TO SIX MONTHS: By now, dominant traits have been established, and sexual maturity is about to be reached. At six months of age, the puppy should be housebroken and understand basic commands, such as sit, stay, down, and come.

CHAPTER SIX

Things to Know as Your Puppy Grows (Six Months to Two Years)

It can be great fun to watch a Shih Tzu puppy grow to maturity. The period between six months and two years of age is especially enjoyable. Each day will bring a new experience for you and your dog. Don't be surprised if you find yourself telling story after story to anyone who will listen.

As pleasurable as this time is, it can also be a challenge. Your puppy will constantly test his boundaries until he learns what is and isn't allowed. The emotional changes your

As your Shih Tzu grows, you will begin to see his personality develop and mature.

puppy experiences during this period will be dramatic, but you must be prepared. The way you react to each change will have a serious impact on your dog's future behavior.

As your Shih Tzu puppy grows, you'll also see many physical changes. Your puppy will get much bigger, and probably won't stop growing until he's at least one year old. He will change his coat, get permanent teeth, and grow more than you can possibly imagine.

The months will fly past. Snap as many pictures as you can while your Shih Tzu is a pup. By the time your pet reaches adulthood, it will be hard to remember what your little bundle of joy looked like when you first brought him home.

KEEPING YOUR SHIH TZU HEALTHY

To keep your Shih Tzu in good health, you should take him to the vet on a regular basis. Between six months and two years of age, your pet should visit the vet at least three times: once for a six-month wellness exam, once for a one-year wellness exam, and once for a two-year wellness exam.

On each visit, your vet will examine your Shih Tzu for any unusual bumps and lumps. Eyes, ears, teeth, and other internal organs will be checked as well. It's much easier, not to mention less expensive, to prevent serious medical problems before they occur. Regular trips to the vet, along with vaccinations, parasite prevention, and constant vigilance on your part, will ensure your Shih Tzu's health.

If you ever notice that your Shih Tzu is listless or showing signs of illness, such as repeated vomiting, diarrhea, or coughing, you should contact the vet immediately. These symptoms may indicate the presence of parasites or disease. By acting quickly, you can prevent your pet from becoming seriously ill.

VACCINATION SCHEDULE

By six months of age, your puppy should have received immunizing doses of distemper, hepatitis, leptospirosis, parvovirus, and parainfluenza. Other vaccinations may have been given as well, depending on the area in which you live. Most vaccination programs will require a booster shot for your puppy at one year of age, and once every year after that.

Rabies vaccinations will also be needed. The first is usually given at three or six months of age, depending on the laws where you live and your vet's vaccination protocol. A follow-up shot is sometimes given one year later, and then every three years for the rest of the dog's life. Your vet will probably send out reminders every time another vaccine is needed, but you should keep track on your own nevertheless.

PARASITE CONTROL

Internal and external parasites can cause serious medical problems for your pet and for your family. To keep everyone in good health, you should do your best to prevent the following internal and external parasites:

FLEAS: Fleas are vicious little parasites. They clamp onto your Shih Tzu's hair and can lay as many as 100 eggs on a daily basis. The eggs hatch quickly, which means it won't take long for your pet and your home to become completely infested. The worst part is the effect fleas have on your Shih Tzu. Fleabites will make him very itchy, and may open the way for numerous health problems. For example, some dogs are allergic to flea saliva and will develop terrible skin rashes when bitten. If your Shih Tzu swallows fleas while biting his itching skin, tapeworm infestation may result. Fleabites can also lead to the transmission of tapeworm. Severe flea infestations have the potential to cause hair loss and anemia.

As you can imagine, fleas and the problems they cause can be a nightmare to eliminate. For this reason, it's a good idea for Shih Tzu owners to look into some of the flea prevention products that are on the market. Your veterinarian may recommend particular products as well.

TICKS: Ticks are often found in hot and humid areas. They are not as common as fleas, but they can cause just as much trouble. Ticks carry Lyme disease, spotted fever, and many other diseases. These parasites are generally controlled and prevented the same way fleas are. Your Shih Tzu can also be vaccinated for Lyme disease for extra protection.

If you ever see a tick on your dog, you should remove it immediately. Using tweezers, grab the tick as close to your Shih Tzu's skin as possible and pull straight out, using steady pressure. (If you yank the tick out, the head may remain

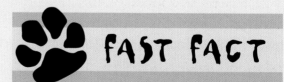

FAST FACT

If you have a flea infestation, you need to treat both your pet and your home. If you don't get rid of the eggs and larvae, which don't require a host, you'll never get rid of the fleas completely.

embedded in the skin, and can become infected.) Then, apply antiseptic ointment to the bite area.

MITES: Mites are external parasites, just as fleas and ticks are. There are several types of mites that attack dogs. All cause some form of mange. Certain types of mange, such as sarcoptic mange (scabies), are extremely contagious and can be passed to other animals, as well as humans. In nearly every case, your dog will itch like crazy. Hair loss, dandruff, and dry skin may also occur. The most severe mite infestations can cause serious medical problems. If caught early, every form of mange is treatable by veterinarians.

TAPEWORMS: Various species of tapeworms can come from uncooked meat and fish, but the usual cause of this internal parasite is fleas. Fleas carry tapeworm and can transmit the parasite to your dog. The tapeworm cycle begins as soon as your dog swallows a flea. Tapeworms aren't usually life-threatening for dogs, but they can cause problems like weight loss and weakness from lack of nutrition. If your dog begins losing weight, or if you see evidence of tapeworm in your dog's stool, such as white spots embedded in the stool, you should contact your vet

FAST FACT

You should weigh your Shih Tzu on a regular basis. Weight loss could be a symptom of parasites or illness. Dramatic weight gain could signal that you're feeding your pet too many treats.

immediately for the appropriate worm medication. You should also treat your dog and home for fleas to prevent the return of tapeworms.

HEARTWORMS: Heartworms are very common in many areas of the country, and are transmitted to your dog by infected mosquitoes. These internal parasites set up shop in your dog's heart and lungs. If your Shih Tzu is affected by heartworms, he may appear weak, lose weight, or have a serious cough. Left untreated, heartworms can cause death. There are ways to prevent heartworms, but the preventative medicines can compromise a Shih Tzu's immune system. Talk to your vet to determine whether or not you should give your pet preventative medication.

ROUNDWORMS: Roundworms are internal parasites commonly transmitted from mother to puppy, but they can also be contracted if a dog

THE DANGER OF HEARTWORMS

Heartworms are a concern for all dog owners. The graphic above illustrates the cycle of heartworm development. When a mosquito (1) bites a Shih Tzu, it can inject microfilaria into his bloodstream. The microfilaria travel through the bloodstream to the heart (2), where they grow into heartworms (3) and multiply, clogging the dog's heart. If left untreated, heartworms can kill.

comes into contact with soil or feces that is infested with eggs. Roundworms can be fatal to puppies, and may cause serious problems in adult dogs. They can infect people, too. There are no guaranteed preventative medicines, so you should get your Shih Tzu tested for roundworms on an annual basis. If you notice any spaghetti-like worms in your pet's feces, contact your vet right away.

HOOKWORMS: Like roundworms, hookworms are internal parasites that can be transmitted from mother to puppy, and contracted through exposure to contaminated soil or feces. Hookworms can cause serious anemia and diarrhea, and are dangerous to both dogs and humans. Symptoms of a hookworm infestation include dark stool, weight loss, skin rashes, and weakness. Your veterinarian can easily treat hookworms, and may be able to provide you with a preventative medication.

WHIPWORMS: Whipworms are considered the worst of all internal parasites because they are so hard to detect and so difficult to treat. The only way for a vet to determine that your dog is infested with whipworms is by examining your dog's fecal matter, a method that is not always foolproof. Whipworms are acquired from contaminated soil or feces, and can cause colic, stomach pain, diarrhea, and weight loss. Treatment is tricky because whipworm eggs can lie dormant for as long as five years, and there is no effective way to kill the eggs in the soil. If your dog is infected once, it's likely that he will become infected again when he visits his favorite areas. Therefore, the treatment involves a long-term course of medicine as prescribed by your veterinarian.

Parasites are much easier to control than they are to eradicate. Your vet will be able to offer you information on the various types of preventative medicine on the market. The vet can also test your Shih Tzu on an annual basis to make sure he has no unseen problems.

LOSING THE PUPPY COAT

At about 10 or 12 months of age, Shih Tzu puppies trade in their puppy coat for an adult coat. In some cases, this can occur when your puppy is as young as eight months old. When the change occurs, it's very obvious and can be somewhat disconcerting. Your Shih Tzu will become difficult to groom. Knots and tangles will seem to form within a few hours, and brushing will take longer and longer.

Although this can be a frustrating time, don't despair. This is a temporary situation. Most puppies change their coats in only three weeks. Once this stage has passed, some owners actually find it's easier to brush the new coat than the old one.

KEEPING YOUR SHIH TZU ACTIVE

Keeping your Shih Tzu active will also help to keep him healthy. Many Shih Tzus get enough exercise following

Regular walking can keep your dog healthy and will also provide opportunities for much-needed socialization.

their owners around the house, playing with a toy, and walking around outside, but there are others that are all too content to just lay around on the couch all day. If your pet falls into the second category, it's up to you to make sure he gets enough exercise.

You should walk your dog for at least 15 minutes each day. A longer walk is okay, but be careful not to overexert your pet, especially if it's hot outside. Shih Tzus are prone to heat exhaustion. If your dog is suffering from this problem, he may pant excessively, stagger when he walks, or seem generally listless. When walking your dog on a hot day, always carry a portable dog dish and a bottle of water with you. Taking some time to sit in the shade every now and then is also a good idea.

NUTRITIONAL NEEDS OF A GROWING SHIH TZU

Your Shih Tzu puppy should eat food specially formulated for puppies.

Puppies need a specific mix of nutrients to promote bone and muscle growth and immune system development. They also need more protein than an adult dog.

Giving your Shih Tzu food designed especially for small breeds is also beneficial. The kibble is usually made smaller, and the food contains a blend of protein, fat, and calcium that is good for a small breed's higher metabolism rate.

When your dog is a year old, you can switch over to an adult food. There is no brand that is best for Shih Tzus, but you may want to look for a manufacturer that focuses on developing foods that promote skin health. Adult Shih Tzus are often afflicted with all sorts of skin problems, such as rashes and dry, flaky skin. Choosing a food that contains niacin, B vitamins, essential fatty acids, and other ingredients that are good for the skin could prevent some of these problems.

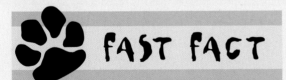

FAST FACT

Don't buy the cheapest brand of dog food you can find. The more expensive brands often contain more meat and less fat, which is better for your Shih Tzu. The health of your pet is more important than saving a few bucks.

CONTINUED SOCIALIZATION

As your puppy grows, you'll need to continue introducing him to new people, places, and pets. You should have no problem encouraging your dog to get out and about—Shih Tzus love adventure almost as much as they love being the center of attention.

If you notice that your Shih Tzu is fearful of something, try not to fuss over him or make a big deal out of it. This will only encourage the fearful behavior. Instead, try to distract the dog with something else. Treats tend to work especially well. Once your dog has relaxed, he may try to explore the new item or situation at his own pace. If not, try again another day.

At about seven or eight months of age, your Shih Tzu will experience another fear period. Pain and fright should be avoided at this time. He'll grow out of it quickly, and without trouble, if you praise and reward him whenever he investigates new situations.

BASIC OBEDIENCE TRAINING

You should begin to train your Shih Tzu as soon as you bring him home. The earlier you start, the easier it will be to get your Shih Tzu to follow the rules. If you work with your puppy consistently, you should have no problem teaching him basic

FAST FACT

Shih Tzus can be trained to do almost anything. The key is positive reinforcement and consistency. Make sure your dog knows what's expected of him, and he'll be eager to please. Having a bag of treats with you during training time doesn't hurt, either!

commands, like sit, stay, down, and come, by the time he's six months old.

If your puppy has not yet learned these things by this age, you must start basic obedience training immediately. Work with your puppy every day for 30 minutes a day. Be sure to break up the time into short, five-minute sessions. For basic commands like sit and down, three-minute sessions are plenty long enough. At this age Shih Tzus have short attention spans. If you make your pet work for too long, he won't enjoy the training sessions as much, and neither will you.

A basic obedience class may also be helpful. In a formal class, you'll learn how to teach your dog to sit, stay, come, lay down, and heel. A qualified teacher will lead the class, and will help you turn your Shih Tzu into a well-mannered dog.

No matter which method you choose, it's important to remember that training a dog, particularly a dog

MISCHIEF AND PUNISHMENT

Shih Tzu puppies are mischievous. They simply can't help themselves. It's in their nature to investigate, chew, and, on occasion, destroy. Their behavior can be confusing, and at times, incredibly frustrating.

Remain patient during these times. Your pet was brought into the family to be loved. If you physically punish your dog or act overly harsh out of anger, you run the risk of turning your dog against you.

Hitting him with newspapers, flyswatters, or other objects is cruel. Praise and kindness are much better motivators.

If you do catch your pet misbehaving, and you want to correct him, firmly tell him, "No," and redirect him to an appropriate activity. This will work whether you're trying to teach him to eliminate outside instead of on your expensive carpet or to chew on a toy instead of your shoes.

that is still partly in puppyhood, is an ongoing process. It will take time for your dog to learn what "NO" means and accept the boundaries that you have established.

In fact, your Shih Tzu will be more rambunctious and rebellious between the ages of six months and two years than he will be at any other age. During this period, he will continually try to show his dominance over humans, and will frequently do the opposite of what he's asked. However, if you're patient, praise him when he does well, and consistently redirect him to correct behaviors when he acts inappropriately, you'll eventually have a well-trained dog.

TRAVELING WITH YOUR SHIH TZU

Even if you don't plan on taking your Shih Tzu everywhere you go, you should get him accustomed to traveling in the car as soon as possible. If he isn't used to riding in a car, he will

Your Shih Tzu will enjoy traveling with you, but he must always be restrained properly while the vehicle is in motion so that he is not injured.

FAST FACT

Shih Tzus are prone to heat stroke. When traveling, never leave your dog alone in the car for more than a few minutes. On a 73° Fahrenheit (23° Celsius) day, the temperature inside a car can reach 120°F (49°C) in 30 minutes. On a 90°F (32°C) day, the temperature can reach 160°F (71°C) in less than 15 minutes. If you must leave your dog alone in your vehicle for a short period, keep the air conditioner running or use a window fan to help provide good air circulation. These fans are available through pet catalogs and in some pet-supply stores.

become nervous every time you take him to the vet or to be groomed.

To prepare for each trip, let your pet relieve himself before getting into the vehicle. You should also take along towels and something to clean up after him in case he has an accident or needs an emergency bathroom break. If he seems nervous about being in the car, give him a treat and a gentle pat on the head. You can also distract him by talking to him in a soothing and confident voice. The more confident you sound, the better. Shih Tzus are very perceptive dogs. If you're nervous, your pet will pick up on the emotion and mimic it.

Never allow your Shih Tzu to run loose in the car, as this can be very dangerous. The safest way for a Shih Tzu to travel is inside an appropriately sized plastic crate. If your pet isn't used to being inside a crate, or finds the confinement too stressful, you can purchase a harness specially made to keep him in the seat. A final alternative is to allow him to ride in a passenger's lap.

FLYING THE FRIENDLY SKIES

Traveling on an airplane with your Shih Tzu takes some preparation on your part. Different airlines have different policies when it comes to pets. Because Shih Tzus are considered to be a toy breed, some airlines will allow you to take the dog with you on the plane. If the airline you choose doesn't allow this, your dog will most likely travel on the same plane, but will not be in the same area as the human passengers.

In any case, your Shih Tzu will need to be put in a plastic crate before boarding. Check with your airline in advance to see if there are any guidelines regarding the dimensions of the crate. You don't want to have any last-minute problems when it's time to leave.

Be sure to prepare your pet by limiting food and water intake several hours before you arrive at the airport.

Riding in a plane can be a long and traumatic experience for a dog that has had too much to eat or drink.

VACATIONING WITH YOUR SHIH TZU

Vacations are more fun when every member of the family is present. If your Shih Tzu is used to riding in the car and can handle air travel, there's no reason why he can't join you on your next family outing.

There are many hotels that accommodate pet owners—all you have to do is find them. As you might imagine, it's best to do this ahead of time. You don't want to be turned away from every hotel you visit when you're ready to stop for the night. If you know where you'd like to stay, contact the hotel in advance and ask about their canine guest policy. If you aren't sure where to stay, there are several Web sites that publish directories of hotels and motels that accept pets. Good places to start include PetsWelcome.com, PetTravel.com, and LetsGoPets.com.

From the time you arrive at the hotel until the time you leave, you

Traveling with your pet does take a bit of extra planning, but it can be a lot of fun and is often worth the effort.

TRAVEL SAFETY

Traveling with your dog is fun, as long as you keep your dog safe!

- Make sure your dog is up-to-date on vaccinations.

- Obtain any additional vaccinations your dog may need, depending on your travel destination. For example, if you'll be staying where Lyme disease is prevalent, he may need this shot.

- Bring a photo of your dog, together with any health documentation, such as a rabies vaccination certificate.

- Keep a collar and ID tag on your dog at all times, and keep him on a leash.

- Make sure your dog is microchipped prior to your trip.

- Don't forget to bring any medications your dog requires.

- A canine first aid kit is a must for campers.

should go out of your way to be respectful to other guests. Not everyone there will have a dog. Take plenty of baggies to clean up after your Shih Tzu, and plenty of toys to keep him occupied. Turning the volume up on the TV to drown out outside noise is also advisable if you have a dog that barks when you aren't around.

TRAVELING WITHOUT YOUR SHIH TZU

If you're unable or unwilling to take your Shih Tzu with you when you travel, you'll need to find someone who can care for him in your absence. The best choice is a trusted friend or family member who can come to your home, and possibly

stay overnight. Your Shih Tzu won't have to be uprooted, and you won't have to worry that he isn't being cared for properly.

Another option is a professional pet sitter. Most will come directly to your home, and those who don't will open their own home to your dog. If you decide to take this route, be sure to get recommendations and interview candidates. You don't want to randomly choose someone for this important job.

No pet sitters in your area? Consider a reputable boarding kennel or doggie day care. Good facilities will have a vet on staff, and can care for your dog, exercise him, play with him, and groom him.

The Web site of the National Association of Professional Pet Sitters, www.petsitters.org, can be used to help you find the right person to watch your pet while you're away.

If you aren't sure where to go, look for local kennels in the phone book or on the Internet. You can also seek out recommendations from a friend, family member, or your veterinarian. Be sure to carefully inspect each facility before booking an appointment. Not every municipality requires boarding kennel inspections. It's up to you to evaluate the cleanliness of the facility. If it's dirty or if the pens and exercise facilities seem too small, you should definitely consider another boarder.

Asking questions about general kennel policy is also a good idea. Every kennel has a different way of feeding, exercising, and grooming pets. A kennel that does things similar to the way you do them at home will be comforting to your dog.

Another thing to consider is the kennel's integration policy. Will your Shih Tzu be put in an exercise pen with other dogs? What about cats? The last thing you want is for your pet to get hurt or to have a negative experience while being boarded.

Finally, since your Shih Tzu needs daily grooming, you must inquire about the frequency of grooming and bathing. Not every facility will have someone on staff who is familiar with the daily grooming and care Shih Tzus require.

CHAPTER SEVEN

Caring for Your Adult Dog

Caring for an adult Shih Tzu isn't so different from caring for a puppy. Pets of any age need supervision, love, and attention. Of course, now that your Shih Tzu has grasped the concept of housebreaking and basic obedience training, you'll have much more time to devote to these things.

You'll also be able to get into more advanced training, and if you so desire, the dog-show circuit and competition trials. Most adult Shih Tzus are up for anything. As long as you approach these new experiences

Your adult Shih Tzu will be up for almost anything that includes spending time with you.

with patience and an open mind, your pet will, too.

Caring for an adult Shih Tzu isn't all fun and games, however. As a dog gets older, he's likely to face a variety of health issues. Exercise and nutrition will also become more important.

COMMON HEALTH ISSUES IN ADULT SHIH TZUS

As your Shih Tzu ages, you should continue to visit the vet at least once a year for a wellness exam. An annual checkup is the best preventative medicine there is. Through physicals and lab tests, vets can look for clinical signs of disease that might not be evident to you. An early diagnosis could save your dog a great deal of discomfort, and in some cases, save his life.

Although Shih Tzus are a hardy breed, they are prone to certain diseases and health concerns. Some of the most common include:

ANAL SAC IRRITATION: If you ever see your Shih Tzu scoot his butt across the carpet, he's most likely suffering from anal sac irritation. Dogs have one small sac on either side of the rectum. These sacs normally empty automatically with bowel movements, but when they don't, they can become inflamed and cause impaction and extreme discomfort. Some Shih Tzu groomers and breeders empty the sacs on a regular basis to prevent this, but many vets disagree with this practice, concluding that anal glands should only be manually expressed when a problem is evident. If you have never emptied these sacs before, you should not try to do this on your own. You'll injure your Shih Tzu if you do it incorrectly. It's much safer to allow the vet to perform this procedure.

CORNEAL ULCERS: Shih Tzus have very sensitive eyes, which is why it's important to check them every day for signs of irritation and inflammation. One of the most serious eye problems Shih Tzus are prone to is the corneal ulcer. This problem can occur spontaneously, either because of a wayward hair or eyelash, or because of an injury. If your dog develops an ulcer, he will rub at his eye and may have a hard time closing his eyelid. You may also notice that the white of his eye is red and swollen, and that the dark part has a small white dot. If the ulcer is not treated promptly, your Shih Tzu could lose the vision in one eye.

IMMUNE SYSTEM DISORDERS: There are several different immune system disorders that affect Shih Tzus. Two of the most common are hypothyroidism and von Willebrand's disease. Hypothyroidism is a hormone deficiency that causes hair loss, a change in skin pigmentation, and lethargy. Von Willebrand's disease is an inherited bleeding disorder that prevents blood from clotting properly. Affected dogs can bleed to death from an injury or during a routine surgery. Simple blood tests can detect the presence of either disorder, and are strongly recommended to enable the vet to make an early diagnosis.

INTERVERTEBRAL DISK DISEASE: Adult Shih Tzus are predisposed to intervertebral disk disease. The disease, which is akin to a "slipped disk" in humans, can occur in any area of the spinal cord. It's extraordinarily painful, and can cause loss of movement and coordination, and, in extreme cases, paralysis. Treatments vary depending on the severity of the problem, and include everything from rest and therapy to surgery.

RENAL DYSPLASIA: Of all of the inherited disorders common to the Shih Tzu breed, renal dysplasia is perhaps the most serious. Renal dysplasia is a genetic defect of the kidneys. Puppies that are severely and moderately affected typically die before they reach one year of age. Shih Tzus that are only slightly affected, however, can live a normal life. If you plan to breed your pet or if your vet suspects that your Shih Tzu suffers from renal dysplasia, there are several tests that can be performed to determine whether or not the disorder is present in your dog.

SKIN DISORDERS: Inherited and acquired skin problems are very common among Shih Tzus, whose skin is almost as sensitive as a human's. Skin disorders can be inherited or caused by something as simple as an allergic reaction to a fleabite or a new shampoo. Most are extremely difficult to diagnose, and nearly impossible to clear up with over-the-counter treatments, so it's essential that you have your pet

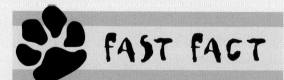

FAST FACT

Shih Tzus sometimes have problems with their joints, elbows, and hips. If you notice that your dog is having a hard time jumping, moving, walking, or extending his back legs, you should contact your vet for a diagnosis.

checked out by a vet immediately. The sooner professional treatment can begin, the sooner your dog can heal.

EXERCISE AND NUTRITION FOR THE ADULT DOG

Like regular trips to the vet, quality exercise will act as preventative medicine for your adult Shih Tzu. At least one 15-minute walk a day is recommended to keep your pet healthy and in good shape. If your Shih Tzu likes to play fetch inside the house, you can substitute this activity for walking on rainy days or during the winter when there is too much snow and ice to safely walk your dog.

Good nutrition is also important. Exercise will never pay off, and may become nearly impossible for your pet, if you overfeed him. Overfeeding occurs when you don't

Playing ball is a great way to give your Shih Tzu the exercise he needs.

control your pet's caloric intake. Anything your Shih Tzu eats counts toward the amount of calories he should be getting on a daily basis. This includes dog food, dog treats, and any scraps you might slip him under the table.

Excessive caloric intake can lead to obesity. Dogs that are obese often suffer from musculoskeletal problems, diabetes, respiratory diseases, and a myriad of other health problems. To avoid overfeeding, you should carefully monitor and control your pet's food intake and keep treats to a minimum.

Most dog food and dog treat packaging includes recommendations on feeding. Follow these recommendations and, if necessary, adjust them based on your individual dog's activity level. Lazy dogs don't need as many calories as dogs that run and play all day.

Choosing food and treats with real nutritional value, as opposed to empty calories, will also promote your pet's health. Most high-quality commercial pet foods contain all the nutrients adult dogs need. These nutrients include water, proteins, essential fatty acids, carbohydrates, vitamins, and minerals.

To make sure you're choosing a good brand, look carefully at the label to confirm that the food is specially formulated for adult dogs. You should verify that meat is the first ingredient and that potatoes or rice is the second ingredient. If at all possible, try to stay away from foods containing oats, flour, wheat, corn, and "meat by-products." These grains and additives have little to no nutritional value and add up to a lot of empty calories.

When in doubt, speak to your veterinarian. A good vet will be able to recommend how much food your Shih Tzu should eat, as well as an appropriate type of food for your dog.

ADVANCED TRAINING

The term *advanced training* refers to anything beyond basic obedience training. This can include everything from teaching your dog to catch a Frisbee and walk off a leash to Conformation and service-dog training.

If you're ready to teach your pet something beyond basic commands

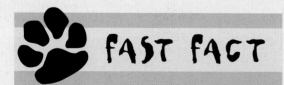

FAST FACT

Dog biscuits and other treats count toward your Shih Tzu's recommended daily calorie count. Try to find treats that are tasty, nutritious, and low in calories whenever you shop for special snacks.

like sit and stay, you can either seek out formal instruction—in Conformation and advanced obedience training classes—or train your dog at home. Training methods will vary from class to class and will, of course, depend on what type of advanced skill you're trying to teach your pet.

Some of the advanced skills Shih Tzus can learn include walking off a leash, catching a Frisbee, standing for Conformation shows, and running an obstacle course. No one skill is easier to teach than another, and all will require patience on your part.

The following paragraphs offer a brief summary of training methods for two of the previously mentioned advanced skills. It should be noted that there is no one method that is right for every dog. Feel free to adjust your technique to get the proper response from your Shih Tzu.

WALKING OFF A LEASH: To teach a dog to walk off a leash, you must first teach him to walk on a leash. There are only two commands your dog needs to learn for this skill: heel and sit. To start, hook a nylon

Only allow your Shih Tzu to walk off his leash in safe areas, and after he's been trained to reliably respond to your commands.

leash to your Shih Tzu's collar. Don't use a choke chain. There is no need to get aggressive and make your dog nervous.

Get the dog into a sit position on your left side. As soon as you raise your foot to begin walking, issue the command "Heel" in a firm tone. If your dog runs ahead or lags behind, say "Heel" again. Keep him at your side the entire time, even when you turn. If you stop, your dog should sit at your side until you move and issue the heel command again. To get your Shih Tzu to sit, pull up on the leash gently, and, if necessary, push down on his haunches.

Don't give your dog too much leash at first. This will reduce the need for you to tug on the lead and forcibly correct the dog. Also, be sure to praise your dog constantly when he follows the command. Offering occasional treats as a reward doesn't hurt either. Whatever you do, don't punish your dog or jerk him around aggressively if he doesn't pick up on this skill right away. If you're patient and consistent, he will eventually learn.

As your dog becomes more and more advanced, you can teach him to walk off leash. For obvious reasons, this is best done in an enclosed area until your dog proves he can behave and follow your every command.

CATCHING A FRISBEE: Teaching a dog to catch a Frisbee can be fun for both you and your dog. This activity provides great exercise and an opportunity for you to strengthen the bond between you and your pet.

The first step is to get your dog interested in the Frisbee. Start by rolling a small Frisbee on the ground in front of him. When he tries to take it, let him have it and give him lots of praise.

The next step is getting him to chase the disc when you throw it. Begin with low throws that are easy for him to see. After a while, begin adding the command "catch" when he's chasing the disc. Every time your Shih Tzu catches the Frisbee, give him lots of praise. He will eventually come to learn that this is a good thing and actively try to catch the disc on every throw.

When he's ready, encourage him to bring the disc back to you after he has caught it, using the "come" command. If necessary, put him on a long lead and give him a gentle tug in your direction to let him know what you want him to do.

SHOWING YOUR SHIH TZU

Your chic and talented Shih Tzu may be a natural for the show ring. Consider the following possibilities:

CONFORMATION SHOWS: You can enter your Shih Tzu in a Conformation show when he's a puppy, or you can wait until he's a bit older and more confident in the ring. Any registered Shih Tzu over the age of six months can be entered in a Conformation show. The only dogs barred from competing are those that have a disqualifying fault and those that have been spayed or neutered.

In a Conformation show, your Shih Tzu won't be competing against other dogs, but will instead be judged against the breed standard. The Shih Tzu that comes closest to the breed standard generally wins, but personality and showmanship can score your dog extra points.

You can find Conformation shows in nearly every country. In the United States, the American Kennel Club sponsors three kinds of Conformation shows for Shih Tzus: a specialty show (for Shih Tzus only),

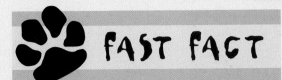

FAST FACT

The American Kennel Club offers more than 40 different competition titles, many of which Shih Tzu are eligible to win. For a complete list, visit the American Kennel Club Web site, www.akc.org.

a group show (for all breeds in the toy group), and an all-breed show (for all AKC-registered breeds).

To be considered an AKC Champion of Record, Shih Tzus must accumulate 15 points at various shows. For a Conformation Championship in Canada, dogs need 10 points. In the United Kingdom, the process of earning a championship is a bit different. The UK does not have a point system, but instead awards "Challenge Certificates." Shih Tzus must earn three Challenge Certificates under three different judges to be considered a Full Champion.

Showing Shih Tzus is not nearly as easy as it looks on television. If you're interested in getting in the ring, you should physically attend several dog shows and, if possible, enroll your dog in a Conformation class. This will help you decide whether you and your dog will enjoy

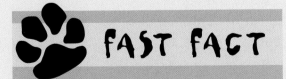

FAST FACT

If your intact Shih Tzu doesn't come close enough to the breed standard to participate in Conformation shows, he can still compete in Obedience and Agility trials, as well as tracking tests.

Showing your Shih Tzu can be time-consuming and expensive. However, many Shih Tzu owners find it to be incredibly rewarding as well.

this activity. You must also be ready to commit to doing a great deal of work. A show Shih Tzu must be groomed daily and will also need weekly baths and training sessions.

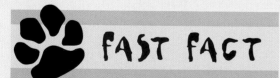

FAST FACT

In the United States, Shih Tzus are shown in the toy group, but in nearly every other country, the breed is shown in the non-sporting group.

OBEDIENCE TRIALS: Conformation shows center around a dog's appearance, but in an Obedience trial the focus is on your dog's skills. Obedience competitions for dogs at various levels can be found anywhere. Those held by the American Kennel Club can result in a ribbon or rosette, as well as a number of titles.

Any AKC-registered dog over the age of six months can participate in an AKC-sponsored obedience trial. This includes Shih Tzus that have been spayed or neutered, or altered in some other way.

The skills your dog will need to exhibit vary, depending on the level of the competition. Some of the exercises include standing for examination, heeling on and off a leash, sitting, laying down for a extended period, retrieving, coming when called, and jumping various obstacles. Dogs at the advanced level will also be expected to follow nonverbal commands and distinguish a handler's scent among a pile of items.

If you're interested in entering your Shih Tzu in Obedience trials, you should start working with your puppy at an early age. The two of you may also want to attend several Obedience classes to get your dog used to working around other animals and people. Finally, attend several Obedience trials ahead of time to become familiar with regulations and show ring etiquette.

AGILITY TRIALS: If Conformation shows and Obedience trials aren't your thing, you can enter your Shih Tzu in an Agility trial. In an Agility trial, you use verbal commands and hand signals to guide your dog through an obstacle course. Courses typically include jumps, weave poles, pipe tunnels, and dog walks.

Agility competitions first began in the United Kingdom, but have caught on in many other countries.

HIRING A HANDLER

If you don't have the time or the desire to work with your Shih Tzu in the show ring, you can hire a professional handler to perform the task for you. Professional handlers are experienced in the show ring, and are able to use this experience to help your dog win a championship title.

Hiring a professional handler is a decision that shouldn't be taken lightly. There is considerable expense involved. If you hire the wrong person, you won't get your money's worth. There is also your dog's health and feelings to consider. You want a professional handler who will be dedicated and kind to your Shih Tzu.

Don't be afraid to talk to several different handlers, check references, and ask plenty of questions before making any final decisions. That's the only way to ensure that you get a handler who is a good match for you and your dog.

The American Kennel Club held its first Agility trial in 1994, and now sponsors nearly 2,000 events throughout the year. Dogs can earn a wide variety of titles and can participate in different classes that offer an increasing level of difficulty.

Shih Tzus must be registered and at least 12 months old to participate in an AKC-sanctioned Agility event. Conditioning and concentration are also essential. To prepare yourself and your dog, it's a good idea to join a training club and participate in

THE COSTS OF COMPETITION

If you decide to get involved in competition sports with your Shih Tzu, the annual cost of your dog will skyrocket, as you add on the following expenses:

Entry fees: $20 to $30 for each class entered. Depending on which sports and how many you compete in with your dog, entry fees for one show or trial can run from $20 to $100, or more.

Transportation: Fuel for your car or motor home to drive to shows within driving distance, and plane fare for important shows farther from home, such as the American Shih Tzu Club's annual National Specialty show.

Lodging: Hotel or motel rooms range from $80 to several hundred dollars a night, depending on quality, location, and whether or not the pet fee charged by the hotel is refundable. At some events, participants are permitted to camp on the show grounds. If you own a motor home

or camping trailer, this option usually costs from $15 to $50 a night.

Meals away from home: Budget appropriately, depending on your appetite and tastes.

Handler's fees: $100 to $600 or more per show. Hiring a professional handler to exhibit your Shih Tzu in Conformation shows, instead of handling him yourself, can increase your dog's success in the show ring, but the cost of earning those awards will increase as well.

Photographs of wins: When your Shih Tzu wins at a show, captures a title, or earns a perfect score, you will want to get a photograph to remember the day. Sponsoring clubs arrange to have one or more professional photographers on site at the show to provide that service to exhibitors. Dog show photographers generally charge between $25 and $35 per print.

practice matches before entering an official trial.

TRACKING TESTS: When most people think of tracking dogs, they think of bloodhounds. But any dog, including the Shih Tzu, is capable of tracking. If you want to test your pet's ability in a competitive fashion, you can enter a Tracking event.

The American Kennel Club holds a national invitational every year, and administers Tracking tests at three separate levels. Titles are awarded to dogs that can complete the Track. If your Shih Tzu can ace all three tests at least once, he will earn a championship title.

If you're interested in entering your Shih Tzu in Tracking events, you should work on honing your pet's natural instinctive ability. This can be done at home or through formal Tracking classes.

There are various methods of teaching a dog to track a scent. Formal trainers will have their own methods, which they will share with you for a fee. If you'd prefer to train your Shih Tzu yourself, a simple way to start is by scenting an object with a dog treat or something smelly, like a hot dog. Let your dog see the object, and then place it several feet away. Your dog will pick up on the scent in the air and find it when he

reaches the end of the "track." As your pet gets more adept, you can begin hiding the object farther and farther away.

Another method involves teaching your dog to follow your scent in the grass. Using treats and an actual object (either you or an item that belongs to you) at the end of the track will act as a motivator for your pet. As with the method mentioned previously, you can make the tracks you set up more challenging as your Shih Tzu becomes a more advanced tracker.

THE GOOD CITIZEN TEST

If you want to lay the foundation for any of the events listed above, or if you just want to reward your Shih Tzu for a job well done, you can seek certification from the Canine Good Citizen (CGC) Program. The program was started by the American Kennel Club in 1989 to stress the importance of responsible pet ownership and well-mannered dogs.

To earn a CGC certificate, your Shih Tzu must be able to accept a friendly stranger, sit politely for petting, stand still for grooming and examination, walk on a lead, walk through a crowd, sit and stay on command, come when called, react appropriately to other dogs, stay calm in the face of distractions, and behave when left alone for three minutes with a stranger.

Although the American Kennel Club designed the program, dogs of any age or any breed are allowed to take this 10-step pass/fail test. CGC tests are administered through a variety of participating dog clubs, community groups, 4-H clubs, and other organizations. CGC programs can also be found in other countries as well, such as Canada, the United Kingdom, Sweden, Finland, Japan, Denmark, and Hungary.

SERVICE AND THERAPY SHIH TZUS

Shih Tzus may be diminutive in size, but there are lots of big jobs they can perform for the local community. For example, Shih Tzus make wonderful therapy dogs. Therapy dogs make visits to local hospitals, rehabilitation centers, and nursing homes to provide companionship and to cheer up residents. If your pet knows how to mind his manners, and loves to keep people entertained with his antics, performing the duties of a therapy dog will come naturally to him.

If your Shih Tzu prefers more of a challenge, the National Association of Search and Rescue is always looking for dogs that are skilled trackers. Search-and-rescue (SAR) dogs are trained to search for humans in avalanches, collapsed buildings, and other disaster areas. Although Shih Tzus aren't commonly used as service dogs, when trained properly members of this breed can assist human companions in a variety of situations.

Despite their small size, Shih Tzus can be trained to help firefighters and other first responders as search-and-rescue dogs.

CHAPTER EIGHT

Caring for Your Senior Dog

As your best friend ages, you'll notice physical changes, as well as changes in temperament. Your Shih Tzu's hair will begin to gray around the face and paws, his sleeping and eating patterns will change, and his movements will be slower.

At around seven years of age, your Shih Tzu will be considered a senior dog. This doesn't mean his quality of life will diminish dramatically or that he'll no longer be a joy to be around. It simply means that as your dog enters his twilight years, he will probably slow down somewhat

As your Shih Tzu ages, the hair on his face will start to turn gray.

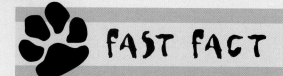

FAST FACT

Your Shih Tzu won't really understand why he's slowing down physically. Try to do everything in your power to make the transition as easy for him as possible.

and need a little more attention and care than he did when he was younger.

HEALTH PROBLEMS RELATED TO AGING

Preventative care becomes even more important when your dog enters his senior years. Your vet will be able to help you devise a senior care program based on your dog's age and health status.

Most vets recommend at least two regular checkups each year for senior Shih Tzus. Each visit will include a weight check, a full physical exam, parasite tests, and a dental exam. Some vets will also perform blood smears, a urinalysis, an electrocardiogram, and other tests to get a picture of your dog's overall health.

No matter how much care your Shih Tzu receives, there are some health problems related to aging that cannot be prevented. Getting these problems diagnosed early and discussing treatment options with your vet will keep your beloved pet as comfortable as possible.

ARTHRITIS: Many senior Shih Tzus suffer from arthritis, an extremely painful and degenerative joint disease. Symptoms can be hard to spot at first. As the disease becomes progressively worse, your dog will move with obvious stiffness, will have difficulty jumping on furniture or climbing stairs, and may even become aggressive when the pain becomes unbearable. There is no way to cure arthritis. However, your vet will be able to develop a treatment plan to alleviate your Shih Tzu's pain using a combination of medicine, supplements, and exercise therapy.

COGNITIVE DYSFUNCTION SYNDROME: Known more commonly as old-dog syndrome, cognitive dysfunction syndrome (CDS) is the progressive deterioration of cognitive abilities. In plain English, this means your dog is getting older and slowing down. Common signs of CDS include sleeping more during the day, frequent potty accidents, confusion or forgetfulness, and a decreased desire to socialize. More than half of all senior dogs have some form of CDS. Treatments include medication and therapy.

HEARING AND VISION LOSS: It's not uncommon for older dogs to suffer from a progressive loss of hearing or sight. Hearing problems are generally caused by deterioration of the hearing mechanism within the ear, and vision loss can result from cataracts or other age-related issues. Treatment may or may not be available, depending on the problem.

HEART DISEASE: Like humans, older Shih Tzus can suffer from heart disease. In some cases, the disease is inherited, but in others, it's acquired. Some of the early symptoms of heart disease include coughing and labored breathing. Your vet can check for cardiac problems when performing a physical, and will be able to advise you with regard to treatment options that are available.

NUTRITION

A senior Shih Tzu has a different lifestyle than a puppy or an adult dog, and should have a different diet as well. As a dog ages, he begins sleeping more and exercising less. His metabolism also changes.

The typical result is weight gain. While a roly-poly Shih Tzu may appear cute, obesity will only serve to compound age-related health problems. Arthritis and joint pain can become worse if your pet is forced to carry around extra weight. Damage can also be done

BEHAVIOR CHANGES IN SENIOR SHIH TZUS

Senior dogs are full of surprises. In addition to physical changes, you can also expect changes in the behavior of your senior Shih Tzu. Separation anxiety is common, as are house-soiling accidents. The barking, whining, and destructive behavior that characterized your Shih Tzu's puppyhood may recur suddenly when your dog reaches his senior years.

You need to be patient and loving during this time. Older dogs cannot hold their bladder the way they did when they were young and they may be ashamed of this incontinence. Your older Shih Tzu may also find that being left alone is too stressful to bear. Bad behavior may also be a side effect of medication.

Instead of getting angry at your dog, try to make things easier on him. Just because your pet is getting older, that doesn't mean that he doesn't deserve your continued love and protection.

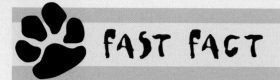

FAST FACT

If possible, stay away from senior dog foods that contain red dye. Older Shih Tzus often have allergic reactions to food that contains this nonnutritional additive, and these reactions can cause skin problems.

to the heart, liver, kidneys and other organs. For this reason alone, you must adjust your Shih Tzu's diet before his weight gets out of control.

Smaller portions are generally recommended, as is a change in what your dog eats. Your older Shih Tzu should be given food that's easy to chew and easy to digest. A diet of lamb and rice or another light protein/carbohydrate combination usually works well. Your vet may also recommend supplementing your dog's diet with foods high in fiber, such as pumpkin, and foods low in fat, such as vegetables and marrow broth.

EXERCISE AND LIMITATIONS

Exercising your senior dog will help him live a longer and more comfort-

As your Shih Tzu ages, be sure to adjust his exercise regimen accordingly.

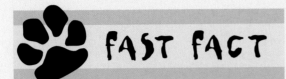

FAST FACT

In their desire to keep up with their owners, senior Shih Tzus often overexert themselves during a walk or a run. When you exercise your pet, check frequently for signs that your dog is getting too tired to continue.

able life. Not only will a good dose of exercise each day help to maintain your dog's weight, but it will also provide the opportunity for the two of you to bond and have fun together.

Be careful not to overdo it, however. Senior dogs have limitations, and there are some exercises that may not be appropriate for your pet. Walking is generally considered to be a safe activity, but if you want to do anything beyond that, you should check with your veterinarian first to make sure you won't be putting too much pressure on your

FAST FACT

Arthritis pain is often worse in the morning or on cold days. If you notice that this is true for your dog, speak to your vet about the best times to administer medication.

dog's joints or too much of a strain on his heart.

Walks should also be kept short. Exercising your pet for too long could lead to exhaustion, particularly if it's hot and humid outside. This doesn't mean that you can't take several walks a day or enjoy romps in the park. As long as your Shih Tzu is up for it, and your veterinarian approves, there is no limit to what you and your Shih Tzu can do together.

SAYING GOOD-BYE

Saying good-bye to a beloved pet is one of the hardest things you'll ever have to do. By the time you're required to do this, your Shih Tzu will have become an integral part of your family.

Unfortunately, very few dogs die peacefully in their sleep. A time may come when you're forced to make the decision to end your pet's life. This usually happens because of a life-threatening illness that is past the point of curing or treatment. If your Shih Tzu can no longer enjoy the simple pleasures of life, and is suffering extreme pain or discomfort, euthanasia may be the right choice.

Euthanasia is the planned killing of a dog by means of an injection. The initial poke aside, it's absolutely painless for your dog. Of course, it

It may ease your grief to review photographs of you and your Shih Tzu in happier times.

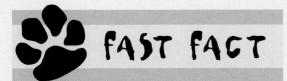

FAST FACT

After your pet passes away, you'll have to make final arrangements. The most common methods of laying a pet to rest are cremation and full body burial. Most veterinarians offer cremation services and pet cemetery recommendations. If your vet doesn't, you can locate a private crematorium or pet cemetery through the Web site of the International Association of Pet Cemeteries and Crematories, www.iaopc.com.

will be very painful for you. Nobody wants to be forced to put a beloved animal companion to sleep. However, if keeping your precious Shih Tzu alive will only prolong his suffering, euthanasia may be the kindest thing you can do.

GRIEVING

The death of your constant companion will no doubt be a traumatic experience. Give yourself time to grieve. If you don't want to go it alone, there are many national and local support groups you can turn to. People in these groups had similar experiences and will understand what you're going through.

If you have other pets, don't be surprised if they go through a grieving period as well. Your Shih Tzu was part of a pack, and his loss will most likely affect everyone in the household.

Although it may be tempting to go out and get another dog immediately to fill the void that you feel, that may not be the best thing to do. A new pet will do much better entering a happy household as opposed to one that is filled with despair. After you and the rest of your family have had an opportunity to make peace with your Shih Tzu's passing, then you may feel ready to get another dog—perhaps even another Shih Tzu!

Organizations to Contact

American Animal Hospital Association
12575 West Bayaud Ave.
Lakewood, CO 80228
Phone: 303-986-2800
Fax: 800-252-2242
Email: info@aahanet.org
Web site: www.aahanet.org

American Canine Association, Inc.
200 Lincoln Avenue, Suite 119
Phoenixville, PA 19460
Phone: 800-651-8332
Fax: 800-422-1864
Email: acacanines@aol.com
Web site: www.acainfo.com

American Dog Breeders Association
P.O. Box 1771
Salt Lake City, UT 84110
Phone: 801-936-7513
Email: bstofshw@adba.cc
Web site: www.adbadogs.com

American Kennel Club
5580 Centerview Drive
Raleigh, NC 27606
Phone: 919-233-9767
Email: info@akc.org
Web site: www.akc.org

American Shih Tzu Club
279 Sun Valley Court
Ripon, CA 95366
Web site: www.shihtzu.org

Association of Pet Dog Trainers
150 Executive Center Drive, Box 35
Greenville, SC 29615
Phone: 800-738-3647
Fax: 864-331-0767
Email: information@apdt.com
Web site: www.apdt.com

Canadian Kennel Club
89 Skyway Avenue
Etobicoke, Ontario
Canada M9W6R4
Phone: 416-675-5511
Fax: 416-675-6506
Email: information@ckc.ca
Web site: www.ckc.ca

Canadian Shih Tzu Club
Jane Couch, president
334 Mud Street
Grassie, Ontario
Canada
L0R 1M0
Phone: 905-945-4343
Email: jcouch@lashalimar.ca
Web site: www.canadianshihtzuclub.ca

Canine Eye Registration Foundation
1717 Philo Road
P.O. Box 3007
Urbana, IL 61803-3007
Phone: 217-693-4800
Fax: 217-693-4801
Email: cerf@vmdb.org
Web site: www.vmdb.org/cerf.html

Canine Health Foundation
P.O. Box 37941
Raleigh, NC 27627-7941
Phone: 888-682-9696
Fax: 919-334-4011
Email: akcchf@akc.org
Web site: http://akcchf.org

Delta Society
875 124th Avenue NE, Suite 101
Bellevue, WA 98005
Phone: 425-226-7357
Fax: 425-679-5539
Email: info@deltasociety.org
Web site: www.deltasociety.org

The Kennel Club of the United Kingdom
1-5 Clarges Street
Piccadilly
London W1J 8AB
United Kingdom
Phone: 0870 606 6750
Fax: 020 7518 1058
Web site: www.thekennelclub.org.uk

National Association of Dog Obedience Instructors
PMB 369
729 Grapevine Hwy
Hurst, TX 76054-2085
Email: corrsec2@nadoi.org
Web site: www.nadoi.org

National Association of Professional Pet Sitters
17000 Commerce Parkway, Suite C
Mt. Laurel, NJ 08054
Phone: 856-439-0324
Fax: 856-439-0525
Email: napps@ahint.com
Web site: www.petsitters.org

North American Dog Agility Council (NADAC)
11522 South Highway 3
Cataldo, ID 83810
Email: info@nadac.com
Web site: www.nadac.com

Pet Sitters International
418 East King Street
King, NC 27021-9163
Phone: 336-983-9222
Fax: 336-983-3755
Web site: www.petsit.com

The Shih Tzu Club
Mrs. P. Gregory Marpalyn
5 Radnor Park
Corston, Nr. Malmesbury
Wiltshire SN16 0HE
United Kingdom
Phone: 016 6682 2380
Fax: 016 6682 7515
Email address:
    marpalyn@talktalk.net
Web site: www.theshihtzuclub.co.uk

Shih Tzu Rescue, Inc.
4474 Weston Road, #175
Davie, FL 33331
Phone: 954-680-6456
Email: shihtzurescue.org
Web site: www.shihtzurescue.org

Therapy Dogs International, Inc.
88 Bartley Road
Flanders, NJ 07836
Phone: 973-252-9800
Fax: 973-252-7171
Email: tdi@gti.net
Web site: www.tdi-dog.org

UK National Pet Register
74 North Albert Street, Dept 2
Fleetwood, Lancashire
FY7 6BJ
United Kingdom
Web site: www.nationalpetregister.org

United States Dog Agility Association, Inc. (USDAA)
P.O. Box 850955
Richardson, TX 75085-0955
Phone: 972-487-2200
Fax: 972-272-4404
Email: info@usdaa.com
Web site: www.usdaa.com

World Canine Freestyle Organization (WCFO)
P.O. Box 350122
Brooklyn, NY 11235-2525
Phone: 718-332-8336
Fax: 718-646-2686
Email: wcfodogs@aol.com
Web site:
    www.worldcaninefreestyle.org

Further Reading

Adamson, Eve. *Shih Tzu for Dummies*. Hoboken, N.J.: John Wiley and Sons, 2007.

Gagne, Tammy. *Shih Tzu*. Neptune City, N.J.: TFH Publications, 2006.

Heinrichs Gray, Susan. *Shih Tzus*. Mankato, Minn.: Child's World, 2007.

Linzy, Jan, and Sharae Pata. *Shih Tzu Champions, 1969–2004*. Incline Village, Nev.: Camino EE & Book Co., 2005.

Milligan, Theresa Marie. *Shih Tzu Files: Questions and Answers*. Morrisville, N.C.: Lulu, 2006.

Sprinkle, Tammy. *How to Groom a Shih Tzu Perfectly: A Step by Step Illustrated Guide for Pet-quality Grooming*. New York: Lifeskill Publishing, 2003.

Vanderlip, Sharon L. *The Shih Tzu Handbook*. Hauppauge, N.Y.: Barron's Educational Series, 2005.

White, Joann. *Shih Tzu: Your Happy Healthy Pet*. Hoboken, N.J.: John Wiley and Sons, 2005.

Internet Resources

www.akc.org/breeds/shih_tzu/index.cfm

This page contains the American Kennel Club's description of the Shih Tzu breed standard.

www.aspca.org

The Web site of the American Society for the Prevention of Cruelty to Animals provides expert advice on pet care, animal behavior, and other pet-related topics.

www.canadianshihtzuclub.ca

The Canadian Shih Tzu Club Web site offers breed information and articles on Shih Tzus.

www.ckc.ca/en/Default.aspx?tabid=99&BreedCode=SIT

This Web page contains the Canadian Kennel Club's breed standards for Shih Tzus.

www.hsus.org

The official Web site of the Humane Society of the United States offers valuable information about pet adoption and pet issues.

Publisher's Note: The Web sites listed on these pages were active at the time of publication. The publisher is not responsible for Web sites that have changed their address or discontinued operation since the date of publication.

www.shihtzu.org

The official American Shih Tzu Club Web site includes a wealth of information about the Shih Tzu, guidelines for breeders, and resources for Shih Tzu owners.

www.thekennelclub.org.uk/item/174

This Web page contains the Kennel Club of the United Kingdom's breed standards for Shih Tzus.

www.westminsterkennelclub.org

This Web site, sponsored by the Westminster Kennel Club, includes details about the Westminster Dog Show, as well as breed information and showmanship videos.

Index

Contributors

KAREN SCHWEITZER lives in Michigan with her husband and their two dogs, Radar and Cookie. Karen has written numerous articles for major magazines and newspapers, such as the *New York Times*, the *Erickson Tribune*, and *Learning Through History*, and for Web sites like About.com and eFinanceDirectory.com. Pet care, particularly care for dogs, has always been one of her favorite writing topics. You can learn more about Karen on her Web site, www.karenschweitzer.com.

Senior Consulting Editor **GARY KORSGAARD, DVM,** has had a long and distinguished career in veterinary medicine. After graduating from The Ohio State University's College of Veterinary Medicine in 1963, he spent two years as a captain in the Veterinary Corps of the U.S. Army. During that time he attended the Walter Reed Army Institute of Research and became Chief of the Veterinary Division for the Sixth Army Medical Laboratory at the Presidio, San Francisco.

In 1968 Dr. Korsgaard founded the Monte Vista Veterinary Hospital in Concord, California, where he practiced for 32 years as a small animal veterinarian. He is a past president of the Contra Costa Veterinary Association, and was one of the founding members of the Contra Costa Veterinary Emergency Clinic, serving as president and board member of that hospital for nearly 30 years.

Dr. Korsgaard retired in 2000, and currently enjoys golf, hiking, international travel, and spending time with his wife Susan and their three children and four grandchildren.